RESEARCH METHODS IN LIBRARY AND INFORMATION STUDIES

RESEARCH METHODS IN LIBRARY AND INFORMATION STUDIES

Edited by

Margaret Slater

LA

THE LIBRARY ASSOCIATION
LONDON

Published by
Library Association Publishing Ltd
7 Ridgmount Street
London WC1E 7AE

First published 1990

British Library Cataloguing in Publication Data

Research methods in library and information studies.
  1. Librarianship & information science. Research. Methodology
  I. Slater, Margaret
  020'.72

  ISBN 0-85365-908-7

Typeset in 10/11pt Palacio by Library Association Publishing Ltd
Printed and made in Great Britain by Bookcraft (Bath) Ltd

Contents

About the authors   vi
Foreword *Dr Micheline Hancock-Beaulieu*   vii
Preface *Margaret Slater*   viii
Acknowledgements   x

1 Planning your project *Nick Moore*   1
2 Working with raw and second-hand data
   Harry East   9
3 Sampling techniques and recruiting respondents
   Philip Payne   23
4 Quantitative research *Peter Mann*   44
5 Asking questions: Questionnaire design and
   question phrasing *Paul Burton*   62
6 Data analysis and interpretation (quantitative)
   Robert Peacock   77
7 Qualitative research *Margaret Slater*   107
8 Analysing qualitative material *Helen Finch*   128
9 Observation and after *David Streatfield*   148
10 Communicating the findings and publicizing
   the research *Jane Steele and Sue Ells*   166

Index   181

About the authors

Paul Burton Lecturer, Department of Information Science, Strathclyde Business School, University of Strathclyde, Glasgow.

Harry East Senior Research Fellow, Centre for Communication and Information Studies, Polytechnic of Central London.

Sue Ells Research Associate, Centre for Information Research, Department of Librarianship and Information Studies, Birmingham Polytechnic.

Helen Finch Project Leader/Qualitative Researcher, Qualitative Research Unit, Social and Community Planning Research, London.

Dr Peter Mann Director, Library and Information Statistics Unit, Department of Library and Information Studies, Loughborough University of Technology.

Professor Nick Moore Head of Department of Librarianship and Information Studies, Birmingham Polytechnic.

Philip Payne Sub-Librarian, Academic and Information Services, City of London Polytechnic.

Robert Peacock Lecturer in Research Methods, Faculty of Social Sciences, The Open University.

Margaret Slater Senior Research Fellow, The Information Research Group, Polytechnic of Central London.

Jane Steele Research Associate, Centre for Information Research, Department of Librarianship and Information Studies, Birmingham Polytechnic.

David Streatfield Head, Information Research and Development Department, also of EMIE (Education Management Information Exchange), National Foundation for Educational Research in England and Wales.

Foreword

The role of research in Library and Information Studies in the past may have been considered mainly to provide a theoretical foundation to professional practice. Although this may still partly hold true today, the challenges of the information society require research to respond to more widespread and pressing needs. The automation of library operations, electronic information sources, performance measures, the need for management information, charging for services, resource sharing and networking, and new information markets are but a few examples of the range of developments in information and library work. The issues and problems being raised in these various areas require a better understanding of fundamental information processes, a more systematic approach to problem analysis as well as more empirical data to form the basis for decision-making. Research and in particular research skills could thus play an important role in making our profession better equipped not only to manage current changes but also to initiate and plan further innovation.

This volume on the practice of research and its methods is intended to encourage more active participation from information professionals. The contributors have been drawn from research workers, library practitioners, and teachers with much experience in the tools of the trade. In aiming to promote a better understanding of approaches to research, the underlying objective is to bridge the gap between research and application, theory and practice.

It is hoped that it will provide assistance to the novice or student who is embarking on a first project; to the professional who is looking for solutions to real problems and to the seasoned research worker who is seeking to learn anew.

Dr Micheline Hancock-Beaulieu
City University, London

Preface

This brief preface is intended just as an explanation of the aims and structure of this book and as a general guide to its use. No more seems necessary, as Nick Moore's initial chapter leads the reader smoothly into the whole subject area, rendering any formal introduction redundant.

Nevertheless, it may be useful to look quickly at two questions: (a) why was this book written; and (b) with what kind of reader in mind; because the aims of this book and the nature of its potential audience are not strictly homogeneous, but multiple. On the one hand, there seemed to be a need for a textbook, usable and useful within library-information schools as a teaching aid and student reference manual. At the same time, it was realized that mature practitioners, under pressure to justify their existence, increasingly want to know how to evaluate their services, and assess the requirements and satisfaction levels of customers. Added to that, established researchers can find recent reviews of methodology of interest as updating input to their work. Various levels and kinds of potential readership presented something of a problem in compilation, particularly as another aim of the book was to be as practical as possible, to teach readers 'how to do it' as well as describe and theorize in general terms.

A few more very simple points should be made about the structure of the book. Use of the index, for instance, is of above average importance, to anyone with an interest in a particular method or technique. An example is that of interviewing, which is substantially treated under two chapters (7 and 8), but touched on in other places in the text. Suggestions for further reading and bibliographical references are not collated in a single sequence at the end of the book. Instead they are presented at the end of each chapter with numbering in the text. Similarly, figures and tables are numbered in the context of the chapter in which they arise, starting afresh with each chapter. Now this is advice on a level of such maudlin practicality that I stand in danger of insulting and alienating the reader. Yet, it may save time in actually using the book to spell such matters out. Moreover, this was meant to be a practical book.

So please, read on. If we manage to help you, in any way, to achieve your research aim more easily or effectively, we will have achieved our aims in putting together this book.

Margaret Slater

Acknowledgements

For constructive advice, support and encouragement, the editor would like to acknowledge the contributions of Barbara Jover and Lin Franklin of Library Association Publishing Ltd, and Dr Micheline Hancock-Beaulieu of The City University, London.

1 Planning your project

Nick Moore

What lots and lots I could tell you of this journey. How much better
it has been than lounging in too great comfort at home.

Captain Robert Scott
Written on his way to the South Pole

1. Setting out

Research is a funny business. It has many of the characteristics
of a journey. There are definite points of departure and arrival
and in between a sequence of activities to keep you occupied.

To make a journey worthwhile and enjoyable it is best to know
why you are travelling. Some people go on journeys simply for
the pleasure of travelling. Most of us, however, travel in order to
get somewhere. In either case, it helps greatly to have a clear
idea of your objective and the purpose for the journey.

It also helps to know something about the overall geography
of the country over which you will be travelling. Not only does
this make the journey more pleasurable but it helps you to
recognize the main features of the terrain and to understand
their significance.

Some people, when they embark on a journey, have a clear
idea of what they will find at the end of it. For others the end
of the journey may hold a complete surprise. Even those who
think they know what to expect sometimes have their
expectations overturned.

Before beginning a journey it is important to work out how
much time and effort can, or indeed should, be spent.
Occasionally, you can afford the luxury of meandering and
taking as much time as you feel you need. More usually,
however, it is necessary to accomplish the journey in as short a
time as possible. Indeed, a great deal of effort has been put into
devising ways in which we can arrive at our destination in the
shortest possible time.

Wise travellers devote some time to working out how they are going to travel. There are many means of transport, some more straightforward than others. In many cases the traveller is a passive participant, simply being conveyed from point A to point B. In other cases, however, the traveller is called upon to use certain skills to facilitate the journey. It is difficult, for example, to travel far on horseback without some prior experience of riding.

Most experienced travellers tend to keep things simple and to avoid risks. There are, of course, those for whom the experience of travelling is what it is all about. For them much of the enjoyment is associated with experiencing new forms of conveyance.

Having decided upon the form of travel, experienced travellers usually feel it wise to prepare a travel plan or schedule. This enables them to know, at various points on the journey, precisely where they are. It also enables them to get back on course if they become lost and it provides a means of monitoring and assessing their progress along the journey. Purposeful travellers aim to arrive on time. To do this they must keep up to schedule at all stages during their journey. Experienced travellers know how difficult it is to make up time once it has been lost.

Finally, having completed their journey most travellers feel the need to go back and tell everyone else about it.

Aspiring researchers would do well to think of themselves as travellers about to embark on a journey, perhaps even a voyage of discovery.

2. Knowing where you are going and why
Successful research, like successful travel, begins with a clear statement of where you are going and why. First, it is necessary to know why you are doing the research. There are two main types of research, one is concerned with the means, the other with the ends. Academic research is essentially concerned with the means to the end. Researchers are usually most interested in the process of research, in developing skills and, perhaps, in expanding the range of research techniques with which they are familiar. To that extent the research process is of equal, if not greater interest than the result which will be obtained.

On the other hand, applied professional researchers are much more concerned with the results they hope to find. For them, the research methodologies or techniques are simply a means to the end. They will be concerned to use techniques with which they are familiar and which are most likely to achieve the required result in the time available and within the precision constraints demanded. In terms of our analogy, academic researchers are interested in the journey, professional researchers are interested in the destination.

Having established why you are going to do the research the next step is to articulate precisely what it is that you are going to investigate and what you hope to achieve. This is frequently the most difficult part in the whole research process. It is also the most important element in designing successful research projects.

It should be possible to express the essence of the research in one clear unambiguous sentence. This sentence should encapsulate what the research is all about and define the boundaries of the problem which is being explored. If it is not possible to express the overall aim in this way then the matter either requires more thought and preliminary clarification, or the problem itself needs simplifying or breaking down into its component parts.

It is impossible to overemphasize the need to establish and to articulate a clear objective for research projects. Unless everyone concerned with the exercise is clear from the outset what is involved then the prospects of having an enjoyable journey are remote.

Once the overall aim of the research has been expressed it is possible to break that down into various stages or component parts and to express these as objectives, or things which the research will achieve on its way to the final destination.

Expressing these objectives, or defining these stages on the journey, is just as important as articulating a clear aim. The objectives will provide the basis for deciding upon the research methodologies to be used; they will form the framework for calculating the time and other costs associated with the project, and they will be the means by which the progress of the research is monitored.

3. Knowing the geography
To make research both enjoyable and productive it is usually necessary to know something about the subject being investigated. This becomes difficult in the case of basic research. Werner Von Braun said: 'Basic research is when I'm doing what I don't know what I'm doing.' All research should aim to discover new facts and new relationships. Basic research, however, goes one stage further and investigates areas about which very little is known. Even here it is necessary to have a fairly detailed understanding of the context within which the research is taking place.

The need to understand the subject is, probably, the most significant reason why some of the best research is carried out by people who would not regard themselves as professional researchers. There is very great scope for practitioners to carry out good research despite all the claims to the contrary that are often made by academic and applied professional researchers.

When the geography of the subject to be researched is not wholly familiar to the researcher it is necessary to make good the deficiency by fairly extensive reading around the subject. In doing this it is particularly important to read up the results of other research into the topic as this can provide valuable clues to the methodologies which are most likely to be successful.

The subject knowledge will be important when you are evaluating your findings. You will always need to put the results of your research into context and to assess them accordingly. Knowledge of the subject, however, is also important during the research. In any research project, as in any journey, a number of interesting by-ways will appear and unless you understand the context within which you are working you will be unable to distinguish those which are worth exploring from those which lead to a dead end.

One way of making good a deficiency in your knowledge of the subject is to involve a number of experts either individually or as a steering group for the research. This arrangement succeeds best when they are genuinely involved in the research and, as a consequence, allowed to steer the project. All too often researchers devote much time and effort towards ensuring that steering committees have no influence at all on the progress of the research.

4. Evaluating the time and effort
For most of us enjoyable travel takes time. A leisurely pace and the opportunity to experience and reflect upon the country through which we are passing are important elements of the journey. Speed up that pace and we miss seeing a great deal.

Research is much like this. It is, however, necessary to draw a balance between the pleasure of the journey and the reward of the arrival. Quite simply, leisurely research, just like leisurely travel, is expensive and in most cases the cost is difficult to justify in terms of the purpose of the exercise.

In many cases, it is more worthwhile to make a quick sortie and to spend a very brief time exploring the place you want to visit. You may not be able to do more than have a quick glance at the main features or landmarks but even that quick exploration should provide you with a basis for deciding whether you want to go back at some future date and spend more time getting to know the place in more detail.

Bargain breaks like this have become an important part of the travel industry in the 1980s and they also have their place in research. In the trade such bargain breaks are known by the rather less attractive term 'quick and dirty research'. Some of us, indeed, have been described as 'quick and dirty merchants'. The rather derogatory use of the term, however, should not obscure the value of this type of research. In many cases, a piece of quick and dirty research can provide the answer to a problem or the information necessary to plan a more effective and more detailed investigation.

Where resources significantly limit the amount of time and effort that can be spent on a piece of research it is worth considering the use of external sponsorship. This can come in many different forms almost all of which require the submission of an application and a proposal to a funding body. This submission is then usually followed by a protracted period of negotiation and inaction before a decision is taken on whether or not to make the resources available.

Obtaining sponsorship or funding for research really can be very time consuming and it is something which really should only be considered for major pieces of work.

Not only is the obtaining of research funds time consuming, it can also place significant constraints on the nature of the project itself. Funding is usually only available, for example, for projects which are novel, generalizable and non-contentious. Funding bodies also have a tendency to place specific requirements on the research process and limitations on the dissemination of any results which may be obtained.

5. Means of transport

Research techniques, just like means of transport, are many and various. Some are suitable for mass transit and are applicable in most circumstances, others have specific applications. The use of kayaks and camels, for example, is recommended only in those parts of the world where climatic conditions are appropriate.

It is often useful to combine more than one research technique. For example, postal questionnaire based surveys can often be usefully followed up by in-depth structured interviews. Experienced researchers, however, usually limit the number of research techniques used on any particular project to keep things simple.

As we noted at the beginning of this chapter, research is a funny business. Once a research project has got underway it becomes difficult to control and to manage. The more different techniques that are used the more difficult the project becomes to handle. Equally, experienced researchers tend to use with caution research techniques with which they are unfamiliar. Only the foolhardy would attempt to cross the Sahara on a camel without prior experience. The same goes for some research techniques. This brings us back to the purpose of the research. If the intention is to undertake research for its own sake then there is obviously much scope in the choice of techniques. If, on the other hand, the intention is to produce answers to problems then it is much more sensible to stick to a limited, and familiar, range of techniques.

6. Prepare a plan

Good research projects require good research proposals. Some people have formed a view that research proposals are only necessary when applying to funding bodies. This reflects a very limited view of the purpose of research proposals. A good research proposal will help to ensure the quality of the research in a number of different ways. To begin with, it will aid greatly the planning of the research; the discipline imposed by having to set down thoughts on paper ensures that all the stages of the research are considered and that allowance is made for every eventuality which can be foreseen.

Once the research has begun the project will build up its own momentum and it is very easy for the general direction to become lost. A good proposal will help to put things into context and to provide a basis for monitoring progress.

There also comes a time in most research projects when the researcher feels like giving up in despair. This is the point at which everything seems so complex that a project ten times the size of the one in progress would not begin to get to the heart of the matter. At the same time everything appears to be so blindingly obvious that it is hard to work out why you embarked on the topic in the first place. Such contradictory feelings are quite common and are easily recognized by those with experience of research. What a good proposal does is to provide an opportunity to go back to the aims and objectives of the project, to the context within which the research is taking place and to the rationale for the techniques being used and in this way to mitigate, if not dispel, the feelings of confusion and uncertainty.

A good proposal will also serve to demonstrate your understanding and competence to any funding organization from which you seek resources.

An essential part of the proposal is a costing for the research. The starting point for any costing is a calculation of the number of days' work which will be required for the research. To make this calculation it is necessary to go back to the aim and objectives of the research and to assess how much time will be required to achieve each objective using the methods chosen. Accurate calculation of the time required is simply a matter of experience.

Once the time required for each stage of the research has been calculated, an overall picture of the scale of the project emerges. At this stage allowance should be made for other tasks such as the dissemination of results, meetings of steering committees and so on.

Most research is labour intensive and thus when the number of days' work have been calculated you will have a fairly clear idea of the cost of the project. Other cost elements can be divided into those which recur throughout the project and those which are once off. Postage, copying, travel and subsistence are, for example, recurrent costs while the purchase of major items of equipment or software are once-off costs.

It is worth going through this costing exercise even if external funding is not being sought as it is important to know just what the research entails.

7. Aim to arrive on time

Completion of research to a deadline is usually crucial. It is important to recognize, therefore, that it is very difficult to catch up time that has been lost. To minimize the chances of this it is necessary to work out some sort of schedule for the research. The basis for this is usually the objectives of the research. For each objective it should be possible to calculate the number of days' work involved and also to assess the elapsed time over which the activity will take place. A postal questionnaire, for example, may only take 15 days of the researcher's time but those 15 days will be spread over a period of three months.

Having calculated the elapsed time required for the different stages of the project it becomes possible to set a series of deadlines. Work then needs to be monitored carefully in the light of these deadlines. For a variety of reasons, the work can become delayed. When this happens it is necessary to take decisions about the future progress of the research. It may be possible to keep to the overall deadline by taking short cuts and in other ways amending the future work programme.

8. Tell the others all about it

Once the journey, or the research, is complete it is necessary to convey your experience to others. In most cases, this takes the form of a research report backed up by articles, presentations, seminars and other means of dissemination.

This is an important part of the overall research process as without it the experience remains solely with those who undertook the research. If research really is to be a process of extending our understanding of the world around us then we should feel a commitment to communicate the results of that research to others.

Research shares other characteristics with travel. It can broaden your mind, it is frequently fascinating and can at times be exciting. It can also be very tedious and on occasion monotonous. It will give you insights into the world around you and provide opportunities for you to meet people with whom you would not otherwise come into contact. Perhaps most important, it can be both fun and rewarding.

2 Working with raw and second-hand data

Harry East

Good research is founded on reliable data. Often, a large proportion of a researcher's time is spent in designing techniques for obtaining data appropriate to his investigations. Much of the content of this volume is concerned with the methodology of data collection and a common characteristic of the various methods is an attempt to operate, as far as is possible, in a 'clinical' situation where the researcher can gather precise information in a controlled environment. Such an approach require that the needed data sources are ultimately, if not necessarily easily, accessible. It also implies that the researcher has adequate time and other necessary resources to be rigorous in his or her data-gathering activities.

In real life researchers often have to work within uncontrollable restraints. They may be unable, for a variety of reasons – such as excessive costs, or the urgency of the situation – to collect the essential data. Fortunately it is sometimes possible to identify and re-work pre-existing data that has been compiled by others having quite different objectives. However, using second-hand data has its dangers. The investigator has to be confident about its provenance: where it came from, the manner of its collection, its scope and the validity of its organization and presentation.

This chapter focuses on the use of raw and second-hand data in research. As this is essentially an opportunist activity, it is hardly possible to present it in a methodical way. In such circumstances, what this author can best do is to review some examples (mostly related to his own experience) of situations in which existing data has been used as raw input for research, and the rewards and penalties of short-cutting the data-collection stage in this way.

High in the pantheon of exploiters of unsuspected data sources must be Francis Galton, a 19th-century mathematician, scientist and sceptic. He was intrigued with the notion of evaluating the efficacy of prayer. There being no acceptable method of collecting data directly, Galton correlated some unlikely information sources: the longevities of royal families with the size of the population offering regular prayers for their wellbeing in church services. The result – in terms of additional years of life over the average – was a negative number. Of course, Galton's assumptions could be, and were, vigorously challenged on a large number of grounds, but his imaginative use of pre-existing data was exemplary.

1. LIS statistics – published and unpublished

Published statistics are obvious sources of raw data. In research projects they are often correlated with data that has been acquired through local collection. Moore's report on statistical resources for library and information science, though published several years ago, contains a description of the most relevant ones.[1] The majority of published statistical series relate primarily to finance, but often contain implicit data on staff and stock resources amongst other information.

Some of the most useful statistical sources are CIPFA for public libraries,[2] the UGC[3] and SCONUL[4] for universities, COPOL for polytechnics, and the Publishers' Association for book sales.[5] The Office of Arts and Libraries used to conduct occasional censuses on staff in librarianship and information work, a series rich in data, but unfortunately these appear to have been discontinued since 1981.[6]

A more recently established source of data on public library use is reports issued by the Registrar of Public Lending Right.[7,8] Although these publications stem from the objective of providing recompense to the authors of books loaned by public libraries, they were soon recognized by the library community as valuable sources of additional information to the library community.[9]

Since the inception of computerized circulation and cataloguing systems, most libraries have *de facto* access to statistics relating to library management activities. This information has provided the raw material for much research in the past and will continue to do so. Most of the applications have been fairly obvious and need not be further elaborated here. Data relating to the use of external services is often less accessible. Statistics on interlending are relatively well covered by the British Library and the regional interlending bureaus. By contrast there are no reliable statistics at all concerning the use of online services in the United Kingdom. The example given below is concerned with the latter problem.

2. Using raw data

Example 1: Using invoices as a data source for estimating online expenditure and use

This first example illustrates an attempt to measure the level of use of online services. Although there is much speculation and 'guesstimation' in the trade press about this phenomenon, there is very little hard, critically assessed data. The root of the problem is commercial confidentiality. Suppliers of online services certainly know the volume of use of their facilities, who the password-holders are and where they are located, but these facts largely remain trade secrets.

Before examining techniques that have been used to circumvent this problem, it might be instructive to consider what sort of data would be relevant, if it were obtainable. What are the parameters of use: the number of searches, this number multiplied by the duration of an average search, or some other measure(s)? In this context (as in many others relating to information transfer) 'use' is a difficult concept to define precisely.

Most of the public utilities supplied to our homes and workplaces (e.g. gas, electricity, water) are measured in terms of consumption, and costed on this basis. By contrast, telecommunications services, which require high capital investment, but consume very little that is tangible, base their tariffs on much more arbitrary measures such as the time a channel is occupied, or the quantity of data transmitted. Similarly, providers of online services, who clearly incur costs and need revenues, have to create arbitrary pricing formulas. Pricing structures vary from supplier to supplier and are being modified as the technology of information delivery develops. But in the final analysis both suppliers and users of online services are mainly aware of the *revenue* and *expenditure* associated with online activities. However they might be determined, these cash flows are generally considered to be correlatives of 'use' and have the additional virtue of being measurable.

To circumvent trade secrecy about revenues, Martha Williams[10] pioneered a technique based on the more accessible data related to user expenditure. The essence of her method is to recruit a statistically representative panel of user institutions of online services in the United States (to which her investigations apply). From the panel she collects information on online expenditure on a continuing basis. The form in which information is collected is as photocopies of invoices sent to the panel members by service suppliers. Subsequently the annual expenditure of this panel is scaled up to provide an estimate of the total national expenditure. (Note that it is not possible to obtain estimates of national *revenues* in this way. In the operation of online services national boundaries are virtually transparent, so that suppliers receive income from a worldwide market of users.)

An extension of Williams' technique has been used at the Polytechnic of Central London (PCL) in an attempt to perform, in the UK context, a similar but finer analysis of online use.[11] In both the Williams and the PCL investigations the basic data extracted from invoices are:

● the password-holding institution
● the calendar month of use
● the hosts used
● the databases used
● charges made (a) for host services in general (b) related to specific database use.

The extracted data are stored in computer files, in this case in the form of spreadsheets. In this form, data from a large number of invoices can be aggregated into summary tables. Fig. 2.1.

The PCL method has extended the possibilities of analysis (at an additional cost) by enriching the records in the following ways:

1. Coding each password holder as a member of an *institutional class*, e.g. university, public library authority;

2. Coding the subject area covered by each of the databases into the following broad classes: (a) science, technology; (b) medical, life sciences; (c) patents, trademarks; (d) social sciences, humanities; (e) legal, government; (f) business, industry; (g) current affairs; (h) general reference;

3. Coding the *country of origin* of each database, e.g. UK, Canada;

4. Coding the *producing organization* of the database, e.g. Reuters, National Library of Medicine.

Thus, by using data created for a highly specific purpose (i.e. to justify host's charges) and enhancing it, it is possible to provide national estimates for a number of important characteristics of the online market which include the total expenditure of a particular user group (e.g. universities) on specific hosts or specific databases broken down as listed below:

(a) expenditures related to databases in specific subject areas (e.g. law, medicine);

FILE NO.	FILE NAME RATE PER HR/PRINT		CONNECT HOURS	NUMBER OF PRINTS	NUMBER BILLED TYPES	CONNECT HOURS COST	PRINT TYPE COST	TOTAL COST
	YOUR ORDER NO.	OUR ORDER NO. USER NO.					BILLING PERIOD 03/01/88 TO 03/31/88	
1	ERIC	$ 30.00/$ 0.14	0.372	0	0	11.160	0.00	11.160
11	PSYCINFO	$ 55.00/$ 0.20	0.679	28	23	37.345	13.65	50.995
13	INSPEC	$111.00/$ 0.60	0.651	146	17	72.261	96.78	169.041
37	SOCIOLOGICAL ABS	$ 60.00/$ 0.30	0.009	0	0	0.540	0.00	0.540
50	CAB ABS	$ 57.00/$ 0.35	0.120	40	0	6.840	14.00	20.840
53	CAB ABSTRACTS	$ 57.00/$ 0.35	0.040	26	0	2.280	9.10	11.380
86	MENTAL HEALTH ABST	$ 96.00/$ 0.20	0.211	0	0	20.256	0.00	20.256
170	ONLINE CHRONICLE	$ 35.00/$ 0.30	0.403	0	4	14.105	0.60	14.705
275	COMPUTER DATABASE	$108.00/$ 0.95	1.107	0	72	119.556	64.80	184.356
278	MICROCOMPUTER SOFT	$ 60.00/$ 0.25	0.106	0	7	6.360	0.70	7.060
401	BIALMAIL-DIALOG	$ 12.00/$ 0.00	0.796	0	0	9.552	0.00	9.552
410	CHRONOLOG NEWSLETT	$ 15.00/$ 0.15	0.164	0	0	2.460	0.00	2.460
411	BIALINDEX(TM)	$ 45.00/$ 0.10	0.192	0	0	8.640	0.00	8.640
430	BRITISH BOOKS IN P	$ 60.00/$ 0.15	0.073	0	0	4.380	0.00	4.380
470	BOOKS IN PRINT	$ 65.00/$ 0.20	0.043	10	0	2.795	2.00	4.795
648	TRADE & INDUSTRY A	$ 96.00/$ 0.20	0.040	0	4	3.840	0.40	4.240
	USAGE SUMMARY		5.006	250	127	322.370	202.03	524.400
	BIALNET-E(DE)	$ 10.00/HR	5.006					50.060
	SUBTOTAL							574.460
	C1 SEARCH SAVE SBCADO							0.80
	Dialmail Offline Prints							0.00
	TOTAL							$575.26

Sample input: invoice

DATABASE NAME	DATABASE PRODUCER	DB CODE	SUBJECT	EXPEND US$
ERIC	US Dept Educ	US/013/01	1	1863.46
				0
				0
				0
Biosis	BioSci Inf Serv	US/002/01	7	366.022
NTIS	NTIS	US/009/01	8	234.913
Social Scisearch	ISI	US/014/01	1	1333.899
Compendex	Eng Inf Inc	US/006/01	8	4025.998
AIM/ARM	Nat Cen Res Voc Edu	US/119/01	1	0.225
AGRICOLA	US Nat Agric Lib	US/008/01	7	0.507
PsycINFO	Am Psych Assoc	US/001/01	1	970.38
INSPEC	IEE	UK/011/01	8	191.622
INSPEC	IEE	UK/011/01	8	9081.565
ISMEC	Cambridge Sci Abs	US/018/01	8	173.852
ABI/Inform	UMI/ Data Courier	US/012/01	2	4318.791

Sample spreadsheet

Expenditure on public library panel's top ten databases (July - December 1987)

DATABASE	EXPENDITURE (£)	% TOTAL	CUMULATIVE %
JORDANWATCH	2490	7.9	7.9
ICC COMPANIES DATABASE	2110	5.7	13.6
TEXTLINE	1610	4.3	17.9
BNB MARC	1600	4.3	22.2
WHITAKERS	1590	4.3	26.5
INFOCHECK	1460	3.9	30.4
DUN'S MARKETING ONLINE	1420	3.8	34.2
BRITISH TRADE MARKS	1110	3.0	37.2
WORLD PATENTS INDEX	980	2.6	39.2
ACCOMPLINE	880	2.4	42.2
TOTAL (337 DATABASES)	37290		

Sample research output

Fig. 2.1 Estimating online expenditure and use

(b) expenditures related to the services of specific database producers located in specific countries;
(c) growth and decline in the use of specific hosts and/or databases, or of specific groupings of databases (by country of origin, producer, subject);
(d) the rate of take up of new services.

As the technique is dependent on external sources of raw data, and their accessibility, changes in the following factors are likely to present considerable difficulties if they occur:

● changes in invoicing procedures
● loss of panel members
● new services, not conforming to established practices.

It should be added that invoices, though rich in data, are far from ideal as input sources.[12]

3. Using directories

Directories, of their nature, are highly structured publications. This makes them susceptible to detailed analyses and – if the coverage is acceptable – qualitative assessment. (Compilers of the better directories usually state unambiguously what the scope of their publication is, and what they have done to achieve good coverage. Where this is not stated, the products must be inevitably regarded with suspicion.) As many directories are now computer produced, data within them should be increasingly accessible. In practice, however, most directory compilers are mainly concerned with providing users with a few, most useful access points. In consequence, such compilations usually present only raw, but re-workable, data sources for the researcher. Two examples of the use of directories in this way follow.

Example 2: Using a directory to investigate how research is being funded

In recent years it has been observed that the funds for research in library and information science have become increasingly difficult to obtain. In particular, funding from the British Library Research & Development Department has not increased in line with inflation. (This can be confirmed by analysing figures given in successive British Library Annual Reports.) It was thought that researchers had, in consequence and with some success, increasingly approached alternative funding agencies. A method was sought to attempt to assess how effective this alternative strategy had been and to identify the alternative sources. In addition, further demonstration of trends might be obtained by considering the following: what value of grants was being given, to whom (i.e. which institutions), for how long (grant duration) and for what (i.e. what areas of research were receiving support).[13]

Fortunately there is a ready source of such information. The Library Association's *Current research in library and information science* is a directory to investigations, studies, surveys and evaluations recently completed, or ongoing, in any part of the world. Originally its coverage was limited to the United Kingdom only, and the investigation described here was concerned with trends in that country alone. The arrangement of the main part of the publication is by subject (CRG classification). Entries are also accessible through a name index and a subject index. The citation for the main entry contains, amongst other things, the following: subject headings, project title, personnel involved with their addresses, sources of funding and the amounts, and duration of the project.

Thus *Current research* carries much of the required information, some *explicit* in its records, e.g. the cash values of grants, some *implicit*, e.g. the type of institution in which the research is being undertaken (Fig. 2.2). In the latter case this information is contained in the address of the principal investigator.

Using the original printed publication alone can be complicated and error prone if one wishes to count and correlate specific data elements within records. It is usually more convenient to extract the required data first and re-organize them in a separate (computer) file. (In this example the simplest of database management systems was sufficient.) Before constructing the file, some decisions had to be made:

1. To determine whether there had been change over time, three sample years were selected – 1978, 1982 and 1985 (1985 was the last year for which complete records were available).

2. To narrow the sample so that it only represented mainstream funded research, the following criteria were used to exclude certain directory entries:

- internally funded projects
- projects leading to first and postgraduate degrees
- bursaries and scholarships for travel
- projects receiving less than £1000 external funding.

The basic record created for each project consisted of the following elements:

1. Project number. Each project was given a unique reference number referring back to the main entry in the directory.

ZmRnOwf—**Data bases. Information services.**
   Downloading   84/4/866
*   Downloading.
   Research worker(s): A. J. Meadows (Professor, Project Head),
M. Hemmings (Mrs, Research Assistant) at University of Leicester;
Primary Communications Research Centre (PCRC). *Duration:* 1
February 1984 — 30 January 1985. *Financial support:* British
National Bibliography £6,100.
   Following on the feasibility study, [*see* next entry] this project
will assess recent developments in the practice of downloading from
the point of view of users and information providers with special
emphasis on the implications for libraries and other institutions
engaged in on-line retrieval. Among areas investigated are the tech-
nological advances supporting the downloading process, the impact
of downloading on online search services, the financial and legal
implications, including copyright problems, and indications of future
trends. *Further information:* M. Hemmings.

Sample input: directory record

Table 1: Summary of projects and funding agencies

	1978	1982	1985
Number of funding agencies	22	74	63
Number of funded projects	105	228	218
Number of projects with joint funding	4	28	23
% of projects which are jointly funded	4%	12%	11%
Number of projects with BLRDD funding	59	109	100
% of total projects with BLRDD funding	56%	48%	46%
Number of projects wholly funded by BLRDD	57	105	89
% of total projects that were wholly funded by BLRDD	54%	46%	41%
Number of projects jointly funded by BLRDD	2	4	11
% of total BLRDD-funded projects which were jointly funded	3%	4%	11%

Subject area	Rank order by number of grants awarded *		
	1985	1982	1978
Information storage & retrieval (8)	1 [2]	2 [2]	2 [2]
Reader services (6)	2 [1]	1 [1]	1 [1]
Organisation & administration (5)	3 [3]	3 [3]	3 [2]
Technical processes & services (7)	4 [4]	4 [4]	3 [4]
Library stock & materials (4)	5 [8]	5 [5]	6 [6]
Libraries & special categories of users (2)	6 [5]	6 [6]	8 [8]
Librarianship (1)	7 [5]	7 [6]	5 [5]
Use of libraries & library materials (3)	8 [7]	8 [8]	7 [7]

*[ ] BLRDD rank order

Sample research outputs

Fig. 2.2 Research funding

2.   Funding agencies (3-digit numerical codes). As each funding agency was identified, it was entered in a separate file with a unique code. This code was used in the basic record to avoid ambiguity from variations in the names of the agencies and to make sorting and counting quicker.

2a. Funding agency type. A one-letter alphabetic code, e.g. R = research council.

3.   Recipient institution. Institutions receiving grants were recorded in a similar way to 2. above.

3a. Recipient institutional type (similar to 2a.).

4.   Value of grant. For the purpose of this investigation five ranges were recorded, e.g. 1 = 0–£4999, 2 = £5000–9999, ... 5 = £100,000+.

5.   Duration of grant, e.g. number of months.

6.   Subject area. The CRG classification code was used to indicate broad subject areas.

Simple manipulation (e.g. sorting, listing, counting) of the file of project records enabled the following to be determined:

- the identity and number of funding agencies;
- the number of projects funded, the number funded by specific agencies or the number by type of funding agency;
- the value of grants being awarded (not available in all cases) including the ranges of values by donor and recipient institutional types;
- the degree of joint funding, particularly any trends in this practice;
- trends in awarding grants of short or long duration;
- the subject areas receiving funding, from and by which type of institution, and trends.

In this example, as in the others in this chapter, the primary source can be seen as potentially rich in data. But much of the data is implicit and not immediately available for analysis. The necessary steps to be made to procure this availability are, in most cases:

- careful examination of the directory to determine what information is explicit, and what data requires extraction and enrichment before it can be used in analyses;
- creation of a working database in which the information is available in a precise, unambiguous form.

Example 3: Statistical indicators of UK abstracting and indexing services derived from a source directory
This example also centres on information extracted from a directory (in this case called an inventory): *Inventory of abstracting and*

indexing services in the UK (1979).[14] The publication was the result
of an extensive survey of abstracting and indexing services,
presented as an alphabetic listing, together with an index
according to broad subject division, a specific subject index and
a list of authorities.

As published, the inventory gave a broad-brush picture of an
area of service activity that was clearly growing. But the factors
determining this growth were difficult to assess precisely. Some
of these factors, identified but not quantified, were: the
launching of new services by both established producers in the
non-profit sector and by new-entrant commercial publishers; the
impact of new computer production facilities; increasing
demand for information in specific subject areas (e.g.
biosciences). The aim of the study was to provide quantitative
assessments of these trends.[15, 16]

The data elements provided in the inventory are identified in
Fig. 2.3. The following were extracted, amended and enriched
where necessary, for the purpose of the study:

1. Producer/publisher. These were grouped into the following
broad classes:
- academic
- learned/professional societies and institutions
- national government
- local government
- research/development/trade associations
- commercial
- international (i.e. contributors to internationally compiled
  services).

2. Subject scope. Services covered by the inventory were
indexed according to broad subject division. For the purposes of
the study these headings were subsumed under six broad
classified groups:
- E. engineering, technology and applied sciences
- P. physical sciences
- L. life sciences, medicine
- S. social sciences
- A. arts, humanities, other
- G. general.

3. Average number of items (e.g. abstracts) published each
year.

4. Starting date. This was used to calculate the age of the
service.

5. Forms of output. The inventory presented inconsistent descriptions of these. In the analysis, outputs were classed as either

232	Name of Service	**Nucleic Acid Abstracts**
	Producer	Information Retrieval Ltd., 1 Falconberg Court, London W1V 5FG
	Telephone No.	01-437 5362
	Contact	David Leech
	Frequency (Times/Year)	12
	Scope	Physical, chemical and biological aspects of nucleic acids, nucleoproteins, nucleotides, nucleosides and related purines and pyrimidines
	Total No. of Items	54,000
	Starting Date	1971
	Average No. of Items/Year	8,000
	Source of Input	Journals, monographs, reports, conference proceedings
	Languages covered	Almost all
	Form of Indexing/Thesaurus	Fixed terms plus free language enrichment. As from 1978 monthly and annual author and subject indexes. Previously monthly author index and annual author and subject indexes
	Form of Output	Abstracts journal; magnetic tape from 1978

Sample input: inventory record

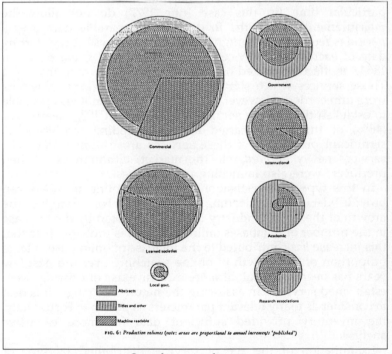

FIG. 6: *Production volumes (note: areas are proportional to annual increments 'published')*

Sample research output

Fig. 2.3 Statistics of UK abstracting and indexing services

(a) abstracts or (b) titles, assuming the presence of indexes in both cases. In this descriptive element, the inventory also indicated whether the output was available in machine readable form. (In 1977 only a minority of abstracting and indexing services were available online, and this type of availability was not then recorded in the inventory.)

As a matter of academic interest, this study was conducted at a time when personal computers with appropriate software were not so readily available as they are now. The basic records used for this analysis were made by pasting entries from the inventory on 6 × 4″ cards. The coded elements described above were handwritten – fixed positions – across the top of the card. All counting and sorting was done manually. Thus, to get figures for the age of services distributed by producer, the record cards were first hand-sorted into producer groups (learned societies, research associations, etc.). Then each group was sub-sorted by the age of the service.

Analyses of this type, where snapshot data is obtained from a particular time (in this case June 1977) do not allow the measurement of growth. To do this, comparable data over a period is required. Although the inventory provided the starting date of each of the services (e.g. the *Zoological record* began in 1864), it effectively listed only those services extant in mid-1977. Those services which started and terminated prior to this date were unrecorded. However, within this limitation it was possible to establish that, of the services operational in 1977, nearly half (46%) of them had started in the preceding ten years. A significant proportion of these services arose from commercial services newly entered into the market, although established producers were also launching new services.

In this type of investigation, simply counting numbers can provide data for misleading conclusions. For example, the growth of the online industry is often illustrated by the increase in the number of databases online. While it is probably true that this increase *has* contributed to the increase of online use, a large proportion of the growth in online searching over the past few years has been the result of more extensive use of existing, well-established services. In assessing the nature of change, it is best to consider as many relevant parameters as possible. Fortunately, the inventory provided sufficient data for more extensive analysis.

Examination of the age of services distributed by type of producing organization showed that in the preceding 20 years 43% of the new abstracting services came from the emerging commercial sector. On the current (1977) rate of production, 52% of the annual UK output of abstracts (1.8 million) was published by commercial organizations and 76% of these were in machine readable form. The 'sample research output' in Fig. 2.3 – more visible as a screen projection than in print – represented an attempt to display the above findings graphically, in addition to tabulating them. The basic measure was the 'annual increment', that is, the number of new references being published annually at that time. This is represented by the areas of the various institutional 'pies'. Each pie is divided into two shaded slices representing the percentage of new references that are described either (a) by title-only entries or (b) by abstracts. A further level of overlaid shading indicates the percentage of each slice that was being prepared in machine readable form. Remembering that this was the period just prior to the introduction of inter-nationally-hosted online services, the reader will note that this presentation indicates that the commercial services (large, with a high proportion both of abstracts and of machine readable records) were poised to take advantage of this new mode of information delivery. By contrast, the academic producers were publishing mainly titles services, with a low level of computer-ization. The probable future levels of market division implicit then (1977) persist in the current (1989) online era.

Other analyses confirmed that the greatest recent growth, in terms of new services, had been in the area of life sciences (42%) followed by engineering and technology (25%). A separate exercise on the record cards showed the heavy concentration of service producers in the south-east of England (66% of the total UK).

4. Final observations

Apparently ordinary resources of modestly structured information can be mined for hard data, or the makings of it. In using such resources the researcher should, however, consider carefully their limitations (interviewing the original producers, where possible) and not attempt to read into the data more than it is legitimate to do so. Data collected from diverse sources is often not comparable, or cannot be assumed to be comparable.

Projects such as the ones outlined in this chapter often demand much effort in selecting, re-organizing and enriching the basic data, but do not necessarily require expensive hard-ware or sophisticated software. In investigating a particular problem area, the researcher should not only survey the relevant research literature (which, of course, should be done thoroughly) but also consider any compilation of information, whether research oriented or not.

Where there is no collected data, and apparently insurmountable obstacles to the direct collection of it, not so obvious, indirect routes may be productive. As one of the earlier examples reveals, monthly invoices, which would normally gather dust in office files, may seem an unlikely data resource for estimates of the value of online services imported into the United Kingdom. But with reflection, planning and a great deal of effort, they can be manipulated to yield appropriate and otherwise inaccessible data.

References

1 Moore, N., *Statistical series relevant to libraries*, BLRDD Report No. 5300, 1976.
2 Chartered Institute of Public Finance & Accountancy, Statistical Information Service, *Public library statistics: actuals* [annual].
3 University Grants Committee, *University statistics: volume 3, finance* [annual].
4 Standing Committee for National & University Libraries, *University library expenditure* [annual].
5 Publishers' Association, *Book trade yearbook* [annual].
6 Office of Arts and Libraries, Department of Education and Science, *Census of staff in librarianship and information work*, 1972, 1976, 1981.
7 Simson, J., *PLR in practice: a report to the Advisory Committee, April 1988*, Registrar of Public Lending Right, 1988.
8 Hasted, A., *et al.*, *PLR loans – a statistical exploration*, Registrar of Public Lending Right, 1988.
9 BNB Research Fund, *Public Lending Right Statistics: Report on a one-day seminar held 24 September 1982*, British Library, 1982.
10 Williams, M. E., 'Usage and revenue data for the online database industry', *Online review*, **9**, (3), 1985, 205–10.
11 East, H., and Forrest, V., 'Indicators of online use. Online Information 88', *Proceedings 12th International Online Information Meeting, London 6–8 December 1988*, **1**, 91–102.
12 Forrest, V., 'Invoices for online services', *Online review*, **12**, (6), 1988, 351–9.
13 East, H., 'Funded research in the United Kingdom. Part 1: Sources and distribution of grants', *Library Association record*, **90**, (1), January 1988, 29–30.
14 Burgess, G., *et al.*, *Inventory of abstracting and indexing services in the UK*, British Library Research & Development Reports, No. 5420, December 1978.
15 East, H., *Some statistical indicators of UK abstracting and indexing services*, British Library Research & Development Reports, No. 5488, 1979.
16 East, H., 'UK abstracting and indexing services – some general trends', *Aslib proceedings*, **31**, (10), October 1979, 460–75.

3 Sampling techniques and recruiting respondents

Philip Payne

1. Introduction

Libraries and information services carry out or commission user studies in order to generate information which will enable them to make more informed decisions about present or future services. The quality of the information, upon which these decisions are made, needs to be as free of error as possible. The criteria and method for selection of respondents are critically important to the quality of research. This chapter considers sampling and the selection of respondents in quantitative studies and qualitative research. Questionnaire surveys and depth interviews may have very different theoretical and ideological roots but there is a common concern in ensuring that respondents are *representative*.

1.1 *Defining the population of a study*

The researcher needs to decide at an early stage who is to be covered by the research. The definition of the *target population* will depend on the purpose of the study. A public library, for example, might wish to assess the impact of the closure of a branch library on the local community. The researcher would need to define the catchment area of the local library, decide whether the study was to cover both residents and those working in the area, and judge whether it was important to obtain the views of non-users as well as users.

The detailed sample design and the selection of respondents can only begin after the objectives of the research have been clearly formulated and decisions taken about the investigation methods to be used. The scope of the target population may be modified later into the *survey population* for practical and cost reasons. It may be decided in the public library example that some of the more remote parts of the catchment area might be excluded or that the views of children under the age of 12 should not be solicited. Decisions about sampling and the selection of respondents are frequently moderated by the constraints of research budgets and practicality.

2. Sampling and selecting respondents in quantitative studies

2.1 *Why sample?*
Studies of users and non-users of libraries and information services do not usually require the participation of the whole clientele or user population. Conclusions about the behaviour and/or views of the whole population can be based upon the responses of a *sample* of respondents. Recruiting only a sample has distinct advantages over a *census* covering everybody. Censuses tend to be costly and time consuming. Except when the population under study is very small or where there is a particular need to involve the whole population, a broader range of topics can be covered in more depth by making a selection of respondents. Studies based upon samples can also be more accurate than those based upon censuses. The limited resources available can be concentrated on minimizing sources of non-sampling error such as non-response, poor question wording, lapses in memory by respondents, or inconsistencies between interviewers.

There is a tendency to think only of samples of respondents. However, sampling techniques can be applied to the selection of areas, dwellings, libraries, books, library uses, or catalogue entries.

2.2 *Introduction to sampling*
The aim of this chapter is to introduce the principles of probability or random sampling. Sampling theory can become very complex and interested readers will be referred to other sources if they wish to explore the theory which underpins the principles. Some mention is made of non-random sampling methods such as those widely used by market research companies and polling organizations.

The words 'random' and 'random sampling' are, as Yates notes, 'gravely abused' in common parlance (p. 10).[1] Sampling on a random basis does not in any way imply haphazard selection. A rigorous set of procedures based upon sampling theory are adopted or what Kish describes as a 'randomization process' requiring a 'practical physical operation which is exactly or reasonably congruent with a probability model' (p. 26).[2] With a random sample, every member of the population has a non-zero chance of selection which is calculable on the basis of statistical theory. Many random sample designs are what are called *epsem* designs as well; this means that every element in the population has an *equal probability of selection*. It is not absolutely necessary to have an epsem design in probability sampling because the chances of selection can be computed and *weighting* adjustments carried out at the data analysis stage. Epsem or self-weighting designs are recommended for all but the most experienced researcher.

In selecting a random sample from a population, the aim is to generalize from the sample results to the population as a whole. This is known as *statistical inference*. The loss from drawing upon only a sample is that it can provide estimates only of population characteristics. As one is not covering the whole population in any one sample, the *sample estimates* are liable to random or chance fluctuations from the actual population values. These fluctuations are known as *random sampling errors*. If one selects a series of samples from the same population, then slightly different sample estimates will be obtained on each occasion.

If a library, for example, wanted to discover the average number of books that registered readers have on loan, one could write the name of each registered reader on a slip of paper, place the names in a bucket, mix them up thoroughly, and then pick out the number of names needed to make up the sample. This would constitute a *simple random sample*. One could then either contact the sample members to ask them or check through their issue records. Such an investigation may reveal that the average number of books on loan per registered reader is 3.2. Selecting another sample in exactly the same way may provide a sample estimate of 2.8. The population parameter, the true mean, may in fact be 3.0. If one continued to select fresh samples, then the sample estimates will cluster around the population parameter in a bell shaped normal distribution (*the sampling distribution of the mean*).[3] Assuming that there is no systematic selection bias, the mean of the sample estimates obtained from taking fresh samples should equal the true population mean. On occasions, an extreme result will be obtained from a single sample purely by chance. It is tempting, but totally wrong, to reject a sample because it appears to be unrepresentative and then to select another. In random sampling, as Kaplan states, 'the represent-ativeness is not a property of the sample but rather of the procedure by which the sample is obtained' (p. 240).[4]

2.3 Precision
Precision is an assessment of the probable accuracy of a sample

estimate compared with the correct population value. Measurement of precision involves the calculation or estimation of random sampling errors associated with sample estimates. Three factors influence the precision of sample estimates and these need to be taken into account when drawing up a sample. The first of these is the amount of *variability* in the population parameter. If all members of the population are exactly the same in every respect, there would be no variability within the population. The researcher could select any of the elements and the sample would be representative. There is usually a great deal of variability in relation to different variables in surveys (e.g. sex, social class, age, educational background) and the researcher seeks to reflect this variability in the same proportions in her or his sample. Secondly, precision is affected by the size of the sample selected. There is a common misconception that it is the proportion of the population selected that is important. This is only the case where a large proportion of the population is selected. The third factor which influences the level of precision is, as shown later in the chapter, the choice of sample design. The art of sampling is to weigh up practical and cost considerations with the desire to maximize the precision of the sample estimates.

2.4 *Selection bias*
Only random sampling error and its limitation have so far been discussed. A further source of sampling error is selection bias. A sharp distinction needs to be drawn between the concept of precision and that of *selection bias*. Selection bias occurs through conscious or unconscious purposive selection at any stage in the sample selection process or through failure to cover the whole target population in the sample. A sample would be biased if some elements in the population have no chance of selection. It will also be biased if others have more than one chance of selection. If probability sampling has been employed and the chances of selection can be calculated, bias resulting from unequal probabilities of selection can sometimes be adjusted by weighting the survey results.

Selection bias can easily creep into sample design. A library is conducting a user survey. It decides to hand out questionnaires to everybody entering the library. On the day of the survey, they find that it is not possible to give questionnaires to everybody at busier times. Library staff are told to give out questionnaires to as many people as they are able. This would mean that the selection of visitors to cope with the waves of entrants at busy times would be purposive. Would it not be tempting for library staff who were distributing questionnaires to favour those people who they thought would be co-operative or favourably disposed to the library?

Selection bias is a constant component of error which is not affected by increasing the sample size. A sample estimate is said to be unbiased if the mean of the estimates derived from the sampling distribution equals the population parameter.[5] The researcher tries to avoid selection bias within the limitations of practicality and costs.

Questionnaire surveys usually depend upon the co-operation of participants. The failure to obtain that co-operation is termed *non-response*. Non-response can occur through a complete refusal to participate in a survey (*unit non-response*) or an unwillingness to answer a particular question (*item non-response*). Although non-response is not strictly speaking selection bias, it can be an important source of bias in sample estimates. There would be no problem if non-respondents and respondents were similar in respect of the survey variables. Unfortunately, non-respondents often differ in significant respects from respondents. Non-response can be minimized in interviewer surveys through adequate interviewer training and good questionnaire design, and in postal surveys by good overall design and effective reminders.[6, 7] Attempts are sometimes made to correct for the bias caused through non-response by weighting the sample estimates at the data analysis stage.[6]

2.5 *Simple random sample*
A simple random sample (srs) can be achieved through drawing out names from a bucket as described earlier. Alternatively, one can give each member of the population a number and then select a sample of the desired size using random number tables or by using a computer program which generates random numbers. Advice on using random number tables to select an unbiased sample is given by Bookstein.[8] Simple random sampling is not widely used but it is the theoretical baseline for considering other probability sampling. As Kish points out, 'simple random sampling (srs) is the basic selection process and all other procedures can be viewed as modifications of it, introduced to provide more practical, economical, or precise designs' (p. 21).[2]

2.6 *Systematic random samples*
Simple random sampling is very laborious especially if the

sample size is large. An easier method is to list everybody in the population and then select every *n*th name on the list from a random start. Let's suppose that you wished to select a sample of 100 library users from a population of 3000 names on the library registration file. The list of registered readers might be in the form of registration cards or a computer generated list. First, it would be necessary to give a consecutive number to each person's card or each name on the list. One would then need to calculate the *sampling interval*; this is simply the total population size divided by the desired sample size. In our example, the sampling interval would be 3000 divided by 100, or one in thirty. The selection of names must begin from a random start, so a random number between one and thirty would be selected from a set of random number tables. From that random start, one goes through the list and selects every thirtieth name.

A systematic random sample is an efficient and verifiable way of drawing up a sample. Although it is an *epsem design*, the chances of selection differ from a simple random sample in that the selection of groups of elements are related.[6] This can occasionally pose some practical difficulties if the sampling interval brings together some intrinsic cyclical relationship between the elements. An information service, for example, may wish to monitor the enquiries received on a random selection of dates. The monitoring is to occur on five days over a five-week period. There are 25 working days over the survey period and these are listed in date order. The sampling interval is one in five. Irrespective of the random start, the same day in the week will be selected on each of the five weeks. This problem is not often encountered but provides a warning to check for obvious patterns in the sampling list.

2.7 *Stratification*

It was mentioned earlier that the precision of sample estimates was affected by the amount of variability in the population, the size of the sample, and the choice of sample design. By selecting stratified samples, the researcher can attempt to reflect closely the variability within the population without increasing the sample size.[5,6] If one selected a sample from the general population, one would expect that about 50% of the sample would be women and 50% would be men. However, one might be unlucky and select by chance a sample in which 40% of the members were women and 60% were men. This would be a problem if it was felt that sex had an important impact on the subject under study. Stratification involves the ordering of the population into distinct groups or strata. A sample is then selected from each stratum. In our example, the sampling list could be divided up into two sub-sets, one of men and one of women, and a random sample taken from each sub-set. If a *uniform sampling fraction* is applied through the sub-sets, it guarantees that men and women are represented in the sample in exactly the same proportions as they appear in the population. Sometimes, when there is a particular interest in sub-groups of the population, a *variable sampling fraction* is applied. This means that proportionately more elements are selected from the sub-groups of interest. The aim is to increase the precision of the sample estimates for the sub-groups of interest by increasing their sample size. This is not an epsem design. Weighting adjustments must be applied at the data analysis stage when calculating the estimates derived for the sample as a whole.

In large scale studies, several *stratification factors* might be used. These might include sex, age bands, and social class in studies of the local community. Sometimes, when systematic random sampling is used, the stratification is implicit in the ordering of the list from which the sample is selected. An academic library seeking a random sample of the students in the institution might use a listing ordered by course. If every nth name was selected through the list, this would mean that students would be selected in direct proportion to their numbers on different courses.

Stratification factors should be chosen so that they are as closely related as possible to the subject of the study but unrelated to one another. If selections are made in the correct proportions from each stratum, sampling error is restricted to within strata. When strata are as homogeneous as possible and differ from one another as far as one can arrange, it should lead to a reduction in the variation between sample estimates and population values (i.e., increased precision).[5] Stratification can never lead to lower precision. The worst that can happen, when stratification factors are unrelated to the subject of the study, is that it will have no effect.

2.8 *Clustering*
It has been stressed throughout this chapter that considerations of practicality and costs often impinge upon sample design. *Clustering* represents a trade-off between economics and the precision of sample estimates. Clusters are groups of elements within the population. Instead of selecting a random sample of individuals, groups of elements can be selected in the early stage(s) of the sample design.

It would be impractical, for example, to conduct a face-to-face interview survey of a random sample of the general public throughout Britain. Instead, one would use a *multi-stage sample design*. The first stage, the selection of the *primary sampling units (PSUs)*, might be to select a random sample of parliamentary constituencies. One could then select a random sample of polling districts within those constituencies. The next stage might be to select addresses and households. Individuals within households would be the final stage of selection in the design. Guidance is given by Moser and Kalton on selecting a national sample of this kind in such a way as to ensure that the sampling units are selected at each stage with a probability proportional to their respective populations.[5] A similar methodology for the United States is given by Kalton.[6]

Costs are clearly reduced by clustering but this is invariably at the price of loss of precision.[6] Clustering tends to have a detrimental effect on precision because elements within clusters will tend to be more alike than elements spread across clusters. Sampling error can be minimized by either increasing the number of clusters chosen or selecting clusters which are as heterogeneous as possible in respect of the survey variables. The equation is complicated though in that, by reducing costs, it may be possible to increase the sample size. This in turn will increase precision. However, increasing the number of elements selected (the *take*) from each cluster will have diminishing returns in terms of precision if elements within clusters are alike.[2]

Face-to-face national interview surveys often require the selection of areas as primary sampling units. Interviewing needs to be concentrated upon one or more localities to keep travelling costs down, to ensure adequate supervision of interviewers, and to conduct surveys within a reasonable time period. It is one of the advantages of postal and telephone surveys that it is not necessary to select areas as primary sampling units. However, even here, it is often practical to select clusters of elements as primary sampling units: an accurate list of the whole population may not exist or it would be impossibly laborious to systematically go through any such list.

Libraries and information units are very likely to want to cluster by date when monitoring use or conducting surveys of visitors. Such samples require at least a two-stage sample design. The primary sampling units (PSUs) would be a random sample of calendar dates. The second stage, the selection of the *secondary sampling units (SSUs)*, would involve a sample of visitors or enquirers (possibly a 100% of elements within the

PSUs) who would be given questionnaires or counted on those days. Selecting only one or two dates as primary sampling units, or even a week, can give a very misleading picture. If patterns of use vary markedly according to the day of the week or time of the year (as they do in most libraries), it becomes impossible to select dates which could be considered in any way typical. The solution lies in spreading out the sampling over as long a time period as possible. If one wishes to draw a sample of a week's enquiries, for example, this does not need to be one continuous week but could be days or even half days spread over the academic year.[9]

Jones describes a method employed at the University of Michigan Institute of Research Library for selecting a random sample of 15-minute time periods over the course of a year.[10] Another approach is to examine snapshots of activity occurring at randomly selected times. The Library Management Research Unit developed a methodology for estimating peak occupancy of study places in academic libraries based upon counts at times selected at random over a fortnight.[11] City of London Polytechnic conducts its *Library In-house Use Monitor* at randomly selected times over the academic year.[12] Whatever approach is adopted, it should be remembered that the final sampling units in time sampling are 'visits' or 'uses' and not 'visitors' or 'users'.[8] The probability of a visitor being given a questionnaire or an enquirer being counted is proportional to the frequency of their visits. It is also proportional to the duration of the visit in a snapshot survey.[13]

2.9 *Calculation of simple sampling errors*
The basic fact that a sample can only provide *estimates* of population parameters has already been considered. But, let's suppose that you have just completed a sample survey. You will want to know how closely your results reflect the true population values. How much confidence can you place upon the results obtained? Are the differences which you observe simply a result of random sampling error?

We have already seen that three factors affect the precision of the sample estimates: the variability in the population as a whole, the sample size, and the sample design. We do not need to worry about the sample design in calculating the sampling error for a simple random sample, although it will be crucial in the calculation of sampling errors for complex sample designs. The baseline for calculating all random sampling errors is that of the simple random sample.

Sampling errors are expressed in terms of the *standard error* of the sample estimate. It will be remembered that the sampling distribution is the bell shaped distribution of means if a series of samples were to be taken from the same population. The true population value ( ) would be at the highest point of the bell and the sample means would cluster around it. Sampling distributions usually have a normal distribution curve in which 95% of the sample means fall within 1.96 standard deviations of the true population mean ( ) and 99% fall within 2.58 standard deviations. For any sample selected at random, we have 95% chance that the sample mean will be within two standard deviations of the population mean ( ). Standard errors represent the standard deviation of the sampling distribution. The standard error therefore provides a way of expressing the particular range of the sampling distribution in which our single sample mean is likely to fall.

The standard error of the mean is calculated from the standard deviation of the sample observations (s). This is as a substitute for calculating the standard deviation of the population values which is of course not known. The equation for calculating the estimate of the standard error is thus:

$$s.e.\ \bar{x} = \sqrt{\frac{s^2}{n}} = \sqrt{\left(\frac{\sum(x_1 - \bar{x})^2}{n(n-1)}\right)}$$

where x_1 equals the measurement for the first person in the sample, x_2 is the measurement for the second person in the sample, and so on through to the last sample member. $\bar{x}$ is the mean of the measurements and n is the sample size. The 95% confidence interval for $\bar{x}$ is established by multiplying the standard error by 1.96 for a 95% confidence level and subtracting or adding the figure obtained to the sample mean.[6]

What this allows us to say is that we are 95% certain that the true population value falls within the range of plus or minus twice the standard error of the sample mean. If, for example, in a study of loans per item of library stock, the sample mean (x) equals 2.0, the standard deviation (s) is 3.5, and the sample size (n) is 300, then we can be 95% certain from the above formula that the true population mean falls within the range of (2.0 − 0.4) to (2.0 + 0.4) or 1.6 to 2.4 loans per item of stock. If the sample size were doubled, then we could be 95% certain that the true population value would fall in the range of (2.0 − 0.3) to (2.0 + 0.3) or 1.7 to 2.3. Increasing the sample size allows us to state the range in which the true population value is likely to fall more precisely. Notice though that, although increasing the sample size improves the precision of the sample estimate, the gain is not in direct proportion to the increase in the sample size. On the other hand, if the variability in the population as represented by the sample standard deviation is lower, then this too will allow us to limit the range in which the true population falls. If the standard deviation in our example was 1.5 rather than 3.5, and the sample size was again 300, then we could be 95% certain that the true population mean falls within the range (2.0 − 0.2) to (2.0 + 0.2) or 1.8 to 2.2.

A *finite population correction* is applied where the population is small relative to the sample (i.e. more than 10% take from the population).[6] The equation then is:

$$s.e. \; \bar{x} = \sqrt{\left(\frac{s^2}{n} \quad \frac{1 - n}{N} \right)}$$

where N is the size of the population and n is the sample size. As the size of the sample grows relative to the size of the population, the significance of this element of the equation declines and can be ignored.

The estimation of the standard error for a proportion is just a particular case of the standard error of the mean. It is calculated through the following equation for a simple random sample:

$$s.e. \; (p) = \sqrt{\left(\frac{p \, q}{n} \right)}$$

where p = sample percentage, q = 100-p, and n = sample size.[3,6]

This is very easy to calculate as it depends upon only two factors: (i) the sample percentage and (ii) the sample size.

Assessments of the probable accuracy of sample estimates are derived by constructing *confidence intervals* from the calculations of standard error in a similar way to those described earlier for sample means.[6] This is presented in the form that we are C% confident that the true population value falls within the range of p plus or minus the standard error of the proportion. The *confidence interval* is again generally set at 95%; this means that we are sure that 95 times in 100 the true population value falls within the range of the sample proportion plus or minus approximately twice the standard error. Setting a lower confidence level means that we can express a narrower range in which the true population value falls but with less certainty.

So, for example, in a study conducted at City of London Polytechnic it was found that 33% of borrowable art, design, and metallurgy books acquired over the course of a year were not borrowed during the first 12 months of their shelf life.[14] The *standard error* of the proportion (*p*) in this case would be:

$$s.e. \ (p) = \sqrt{\left(\frac{(33) \ (67)}{166}\right)} = 3.65 \text{ percentage points.}$$

A *finite population correction* is again applied where the population is small relative to the sample (i.e. more than 10% take from the population).[6] The equation then is:

$$s.e. \ (p) = \sqrt{\left(\frac{p \ q}{n} \ \frac{1-n}{N}\right)}$$

In the example drawn from City of London Polytechnic, the total population of new acquisitions in art, design, and metallurgy was 761. As the sample consists of over 20% of the population, the finite population correction should be applied. The standard error of the proportion would therefore be amended to:

$$s.e. \ (p) = \sqrt{\left(\frac{(33) \ (67)}{166} \ \frac{1-166}{761}\right)} = 3.23 \text{ percentage points.}$$

A multiplier based upon the desired confidence level is applied to the standard error equation. This multiplier is drawn from a table of the normal distribution in a set of statistical tables. Such a table would show that 95% of the normal distribution falls within 1.96 standard deviations of the distribution mean. We could therefore be 95% confident from our sample estimate that the proportion of new acquisitions in art, design and metallurgy, which were not used over the 12 month period of the study, fell in the following range:

$$p \ \pm \ 1.96 \sqrt{\left(\frac{p \ q}{n} \ \frac{1-n}{N}\right)} = 33 \pm (1.96 \times 3.23) = \underline{26.7 - 39.3\%}$$

2.10 *The Design Factor*

These calculations assume a simple random sample and are not appropriate for *complex sample designs*. Complex sample designs are multi-stage with stratification factors applied at every stage of the selection. Usually the detrimental effects of clustering on precision are greater than the beneficial effects of stratification. This means that the use of the above equations will tend to underestimate random sampling error from complex sample designs.

The *Design Factor (DEFT)* offers a means of assessing the effects on precision for a complex design compared with a simple random sample of the same size. DEFT is simply a ratio of the two standard errors:

DEFT = $\dfrac{\text{s.e. of a sample with a complex design}}{\text{s.e. of an srs of the same size}}$

It effectively permits a quantification of the relative effects of stratification and clustering, although it does not take account of the economic aspects of sampling. The savings in costs from a complex design may more than compensate for the increase in sampling error. Furthermore, simple random samples are also not a realistic alternative to complex designs in many surveys. Sometimes the term *Design Effect (DEFF)* is used when considering the effect of sample design on standard errors; DEFF is simply DEFT squared and is the ratio of the variances rather than the standard errors.[15]

Each variable will have its own Design Factor. An index value of greater than one on DEFT (or DEFF) implies a precision from the complex design which is less than that which would be achieved with a simple random sample of the same size. An index value of less than one would suggest a greater precision from the complex design than would be achieved from a simple random sample of the same size. To compute the standard error of a sample estimate derived from a complex design, the standard error of a simple random sample of the same size needs to be multiplied through by the Design Factor. Kalton indicates that in national studies the Design Effect for variables such as age and sex is generally close to one. On the other hand, Design Effects for variables such as social class would be greater than one.[6] The explanation for this difference lies in the distribution of the variable through the geographical clusters. Geographical areas are not particularly homogeneous in respect of age and sex but social class is strongly related to locality.

Homogeneity in and between clusters is measured through the *intra-class correlation coefficient*.[15] In selecting a two-stage or multi-stage sample, the aim is to choose clusters as primary sampling units which are as internally heterogeneous as possible. The correlation coefficient, ρ (pronounced roh), would be zero if the clusters were effectively made up at random and there was no loss of precision through clustering. Collins suggests that the correlation coefficient is unlikely to be less than about 0.02 on any survey variable and can be as high as 0.2.[16]

An estimate of DEFT can be derived from the intra-class correlation coefficient:

DEFT = $\sqrt{(1 + (b-1)\rho)}$

where b = the average number of elements selected per PSU, ρ = the intra-class correlation coefficient.[15]

This equation clearly shows the combined effect on DEFT of the size of the take from clusters and the degree of homogeneity within clusters. Even a small value for ρ increases the Design Factor and it is advisable to allow a value of at least 0.02 in assessing the effects of clustering on precision.[16]

The Design Factor is rarely calculated except for a few principal variables on national surveys. The calculation of complex sampling error is laborious and time consuming although some work has been undertaken on modelling such errors and imputing estimates of complex sampling errors from the models.[15, 17]

2.11 *Choosing the size of the sample*

One of the most frequent questions asked by those new to surveys concerns the size of the sample. The question is not easily answered because it depends upon the variability within the population, the precision of the sample estimate required, one's interest in the sub-groups which make up the population, the level of non-response expected, and the sample design employed. It is, as Hedges notes, 'almost always a matter more of judgement than of calculation' (p. 61).[3]

The textbook approach is as follows. Let's assume that one wishes to select a simple random sample of entries in a library catalogue in a study to discover how many of the entries are replicated in the catalogue of another library. The following equation will determine how large a sample should be selected:

$$n = \frac{z\,p(100-p)}{e}$$

where p = an estimate of the percentage of entries replicated (assume the conservative case of 50% if no idea),

z = desired confidence level
  i.e. if 95% confidence required, $z = 1.96$
  if 99% confidence required, $z = 2.58$

e = number to be added to or subtracted from p to construct an interval.

So, let's assume that the replication is estimated at 50% and then calculate the sample size using the 95% confidence interval (i.e., that the sample proportion falls within a specified range in 95 times out of 100). If we are happy to work with a margin of 10% either way from the sample estimate (i.e. we are happy the population parameter falls between 40% and 60%), the sample size would be:

$$\frac{(1.96)^2 \times 50 \, (50)}{100} = 96.$$

If one wished to be 99% confident that the population parameter fell between 45% and 55%, then the minimum sample size would be:

$$\frac{(2.58)^2 \times 50 \, (50)}{25} = 665.$$

The finite population correction mentioned earlier should be applied if more than 10% of the population is selected.

In working out the minimum sample size, it is important to remember that the precision of the sample estimates depends upon the numbers in the sample at the data analysis stage (the *achieved sample*) and not the number of sample members selected initially. Some non-response is likely in questionnaire surveys. If the expected response rate is 80%, then the minimum initial sample size needs to be divided by 0.8. This will protect the precision of the sample estimates but will not correct for any sample bias.

The researcher is often particularly interested in sub groups of the population and how their sample estimates differ from those of the population as a whole. The precision of the sample estimates for sub-groups will clearly be influenced by the numbers in the sub-groups within the sample. It is important therefore to identify at an early stage in the research those sub-groups in which one is particularly interested. The precision requirements for the sub-groups then become the basis on which one determines the overall sample size. In other words, the above calculations should be undertaken for the smallest sub-groups in which one is interested. The alternative approach is to disproportionately select elements from those sub-groups in which one is interested and to re-weight the results for the total sample at the data analysis stage. The researcher is sometimes only interested in uncommon or *minority populations* and a range of techniques has been developed for these situations.[18]

2.12 *Effective sample sizes*
The *effective sample size* is the sample size needed with a simple random sample to give the same level of precision as a particular complex design. It is simply the sample size of the complex design divided by the Design Factor. Looking again at the example of catalogue overlap mentioned above, one might consider that rather than selecting a simple random sample, it is

likely that a systematic random sample through the classified sequence would be selected. This would result in implicit stratification with the subject range of items in the sample being in direct proportion to that in the population as a whole. If one assumed no clustering in the design, we might expect a Design Effect of less than one through the positive effects of stratification. If the Design Effect was therefore 0.9, then the effective sample sizes in the above examples would be $96/(0.9)^2$ or $665(0.9)^2$ or 119 or 821 respectively. The precision of the sample estimates obtained would be much greater than anticipated. So, to achieve a level of precision equivalent to that of a simple random sample, the sample size need only be 78 or 539 respectively. However, there is almost bound to be some clustering because each entry for a title will represent a cluster of copies. We may also decide the primary sampling units should be frames on a microfiche catalogue. This might well result in a Design Effect of nearer 1.3. The effective sample sizes would consequently be $96/(1.3)^2$ or $665/(1.3)^2$ or 57 or 393 respectively. This would mean that the precision of the standard estimates would be considerably less than anticipated. To achieve a level of precision equivalent to that of a simple random sample, the sample sizes needed would be 162 or 1124 respectively.

2.13 *Sampling frames*

A *sampling frame* is the list from which a random sample of elements in the population are selected. It is common for lists compiled for administrative purposes to be used such as the electoral register, the postcode address file, or listings of students in a college. Published lists, such as entries in directories, some-times constitute the sampling frame. Researchers may need to draw up the frame for themselves if an adequate listing of the population elements does not already exist.

The ideal sampling frame includes every element in the target population once and only once. It needs to be up to date and the compilation date known. It is rare to find a sampling frame which does not have some inadequacies. If these inadequacies go undetected or cannot be remedied, they can be a major source of selection bias.

The first question to be asked of any sampling frame is whether it covers all the target population. The telephone directory, for example, is unlikely to be an adequate sampling frame for selecting a random sample of the general population. Those who do not have telephones are excluded. Telephone ownership is related to various socio-economic variables; those who are aged 65 or over, live on their own, are unemployed, or have low incomes, are less likely to have a telephone.[19] If these variables are likely to be important, such as in a survey of public library use for example, then the use of the telephone directory as a sampling frame would bias the results.

It is not uncommon, however, for the survey population to be defined by the sampling frame available. A polytechnic library undertaking a user survey might well be prepared to accept a sampling frame which does not include short course students. The target population, the whole student body, is refined down to the survey population which constitutes only students on courses which last longer than x weeks. It is acceptable to amend the target population in this way if it does not conflict with the survey objectives and no inferences are made from the survey population to the larger target population. It is very easy though to unintentionally modify the survey population through the sampling frame.[8] The target population may also not be fully covered by the sampling frame because people often have some choice as to whether they appear in a list. Telephone directories do not include those people who have decided to be ex-directory. Even the electoral register is not complete.[20] The gaps in a sampling frame are known as *missing elements*.

A second potential weakness in sampling frames is the inclusion of elements which do not form part of the target population. These entries are known as *ineligibles*. In a survey of the use of new acquisitions at City of London Polytechnic, the sampling frame used was a computer-generated list of catalogue records with record creation dates between January and April 1984.[14] Ineligibles crept into this frame because there were some amended records for books acquired earlier. There were also some entries for material which was not borrowable. The recommended way to deal with ineligibles is to delete them from the list before sample selection.

A third defect found in sampling frames is the inclusion of more than one listing for elements in the population. A library registration file, for example, may well duplicate a borrower's name if a replacement reader's card is issued. If this is not corrected by screening, then some elements in the population will have more than one chance of selection for the sample. Unfortunately, it is not always possible to identify whether there are duplicate entries.

Other criteria which the researcher should consider when evaluating the adequacy of a list as a sampling frame are: the up-to-dateness of the list, the accessibility of the list, whether the ordering of the list is helpful, and whether the elements in the list match up with the desired sampling units. Published lists take time to compile and even a recently published list is likely to contain elements which have changed. Some elements new to the population will therefore have no chance of selection. Other elements will no longer form part of the population. The electoral register, for example, is based upon information relating to 10 October each year. It comes into force on 16 February of the following year and then remains in force for a year. Clearly, as the months pass, the electoral register becomes increasingly out of date as people move or deaths occur. Not all lists compiled for administrative purposes can be consulted or are in a form which can be used as a sampling frame. Computer-generated lists are usually in the form of paper print-out and the software programs frequently permit detailed selections and sorting. Hard copy lists can be written on and are easily verifiable. The sorting facility may enable the list to be produced so that stratification is implicit in selecting a systematic random sample from the list. However, access to personal computerized records is controlled by the Data Protection Act. Printed lists, on the other hand, may be unwieldy and ordered in ways which are unhelpful for sampling. The entries in a listing may not represent the sampling units required for the survey objectives. The elements in a microfiche library catalogue, for example, are usually titles; this may be problematic if the survey requires the selection of a random sample of items in the library. Each title represents a cluster of items. A two-stage design would be required to overcome this difficulty: the primary sampling units would be titles and the secondary sampling units would be copies of titles.

2.14 *Non-probability sampling*
A range of techniques exist for sampling which do not depend upon probability theory. They are consequently very susceptible to bias and do not allow an individual's chances of selection to be calculated. *Convenience sampling* involves selecting those people who are readily available. It may simply involve choosing and questioning people in the street, or, perhaps, seeking respondents amongst participants at a meeting. Volunteers may be sought as in the pull-out readership surveys often conducted by magazines or the telephone polls on current topics which radio stations undertake amongst their listeners. *Purposive sampling* or judgement sampling implies some expert judgement in the selection of the sample. The idea is to select elements in the population which would be considered representative. It

would be difficult to achieve consensus even amongst experts on the representativeness of a large sample selected in this way. For selecting a few cases from a diverse population, however, the method has much to commend it. It might be a sensible way, for example, of selecting a sample of three British cities. Using random sampling techniques in such instances is somewhat spurious. It is like selecting at random one item from a bowl of fruit which contains an apple, a banana, a pear, an orange, and a plum. Purposive selection would give just as good results.

Surveys and polls conducted by market research companies often use *quota samples*. Interviewers select respondents using guidelines provided by the company. They are asked to interview fixed numbers of people within certain categories (e.g. different age ranges, sexes, social grades). The number of people to be selected within categories would be fixed using secondary data, usually from the census of population, so that the totals in the sample in each category are in the same proportions as in the overall population. The method is prone to interviewer variability in the selection of respondents as well as not being based upon any statistical theory. The advocates of quota sampling point to its speed and administrative convenience. There have been some notable successes for the method in correctly predicting the outcome of general and presidential elections. There have been some spectacular failures too!

3. Selecting respondents in qualitative studies
In selecting a probability sample, one seeks to generalize from as large a sample as affordable to the wider population. Qualitative methods, on the other hand, permit the exploration of issues in depth with just segments of the population. The trade-off between the two approaches lies in breadth against depth.

The method of selection of respondents in qualitative studies is arguably more flexible than in sample surveys. The choice of method will depend upon the research objectives, the research budget, and the experience of the researcher. Qualitative studies are typically small scale. The researcher therefore seeks to expend the limited resources available by, what Patton calls, 'purposively selecting information-rich cases' (p. 52).[21]

A variety of models for the selection have been presented. One can seek typicality and aim to represent a broad cross-section of opinion. Some seek representativeness of sections of the population through small-scale quota samples.[22] Others seek unusual, deviant, or extreme cases.[21]

References

1   Yates, F., *Sampling methods for censuses and surveys*, 4th edn, London, Charles Griffin, 1981.
2   Kish, L., *Survey sampling*, New York, Wiley, 1965.
3   Hedges, B., 'Sampling', in G. Hoinville, *et al.*, *Survey research practice*, London, Heinemann, 1978, 55–89.
4   Kaplan, A., *The conduct of inquiry: methodology for behavioral science*, Aylesbury, Intertext Books, 1964.
5   Moser, C. A., and Kalton, G., *Survey methods in social investigation*, 2nd edn, London, Heinemann, 1971.
6   Kalton, G., *Introduction to survey sampling*, Beverly Hills, Sage, 1983.
7   Dillman, D. A., *Mail and telephone surveys: the total design method*, New York, Wiley, 1978.
8   Bookstein, A., 'How to sample badly', *Library review*, **44**, (2), 1974, 124–32.
9   Blagden, P., *Analysis of reference enquiries at Central House Library*, (Library Research Digest No. 7), London, City of London Polytechnic, Library and Learning Resources Service, 1984.
10 Jones, W. G. A., 'Time-series sample approach for measuring use in a small library', *Special libraries*, **64**, (7), July 1973, 280–4.
11 University of Cambridge Library Management Research Unit, 'Factors affecting the use of seats in academic libraries', *Journal of librarianship*, **7**, (4), October 1975, 262–87.
12 Payne, P., *Library In-house Use Monitor – Calcutta House Library 1986/87*, (Library Research Digest No. 25), London, City of London Polytechnic Library Services, 1987.
13 Brettell, S., and Basker, J., 'Monitoring the demand for the services of academic libraries – interpreting survey evidence', *Aslib proceedings*, **35**, (6/7), June/July 1983, 290–6.
14 Payne, P., *New acquisitions, loan strategies, and library use: an assessment using SWALCAP management information*, (Library Research Digest No. 18), London, City of London Polytechnic, LLRS Publications, 1986.
15 Lievesley, D., 'Sample design research', *Survey methods newsletter* (Social and Community Planning Research), Spring 1983, 3–5.
16 Collins, M., 'Sampling', in R. Worcester and J. Downham, *Consumer market research handbook*, 3rd edn, Amsterdam, North Holland, 1986, 85–110.
17 Kalton, G., *Estimating survey sampling errors*, (Methodological Working Paper No. 14), London, Social and Community Planning Research, 1978.
18 Kalton, G., and Anderson, D. W., 'Sampling rare populations', *Journal of the Royal Statistical Association*, **149**, (1), 1986, 65–82.
19 Sykes, W., and Hoinville, G., *Telephone interviewing on a survey of social attitudes: a comparison with face-to-face procedures*, London, Social and Community Planning Research, 1985.
20 Smith, C., 'How complete is the electoral register?', *Political studies*, **29**, (2), 1981, 275–8.

21 Patton, M. Q., *How to use qualitative methods in evaluation*, Newbury Park, Calif., Sage, 1987.
22 Dickens, J., 'The fresh cream cakes market: the use of qualitative research as part of a consumer research programme', in U. Bradley, *Applied marketing and social research*, New York, Van Nostrand, 1982.

4 Quantitative research

Peter Mann

1. What is quantitative?

Before discussing how to do quantitative research it is necessary to be quite clear what the word 'quantitative' means. There are various dictionary definitions but all of them agree that the word 'quantitative' is to do with measurement and thus involves amounts of things, which again involves numbers. As the *Fontana dictionary of modern thought* puts it, quantitative is 'the expression of a property or quality in numerical terms'. So a quantitative expression of a 'long' wall would say that it is 120 yards in length. A quantitative expression of a person's measured intelligence would say that he had an IQ of, say, 150 rather than the qualitative expression which might be 'highly intelligent'.

To be quantitative is to use numbers rather than words, but one must remember that numbers are themselves expressed in words when we communicate measurements to other people. To say that a person is 6 feet tall is to use the word 'six', which should cause no great problem, and the word 'feet' which could cause problems for a person who had only been exposed to metric measurement of the concept of length. In quantitative work, then, it is necessary for everyone concerned to understand fully what the *units* of measurement are that are being used. To say that a public library had 65,000 users in a given year is to express 'users' quantitatively but not meaningfully. What is a 'user'? Do you mean only those people who hold a borrower's ticket (some of whom may not have used the library during the year anyway) or do you mean all the people who passed through a wicket gate that has an automatic counter attached (which may include all the painters who redecorated the library that year)? Even the word 'year' requires careful definition because a year might be the 365 days spanning January to December, but it might also be a data-collection year from April to March, as is used by the Chartered Institute of Public Finance and Accountancy (CIPFA) for their Public Library Statistics each year. It may seem somewhat pedantic to labour the matter of definitions so early in this chapter, but clear definitions are fundamental to good quantitative research. People who decry the use of statistics with such phrases as 'you can prove anything with statistics' or the well-worn 'lies, damned lies and statistics' are often demonstrating their own lack of numeracy or else their reluctance to take the trouble to find out just what the statistics are about.

For years now societies all round the world have been exercised over problems of inflation. Politicians hurl figures at each other to demonstrate how well or how badly a government is dealing with this problem. A decline by one side's spokesman is turned into an increase by the other side. The lay citizen becomes utterly confused. In Britain until recently there was an individual section in the Retail Price Index for 'books' which was one of the categories with the highest rate of inflation of all the 95 items measured each month. This particular item of the index was very popular with librarians who wanted to convince local finance officers of the inadequacy of their book funds. Unfortunately the basis for (i.e., definition of) the actual item for 'books' had never been written down for public scrutiny and when questions were raised about the validity of this item it was discontinued. With no adequate definition of what is being measured the measurement itself is without meaning or genuine utility.

2. Why quantitative?

Whilst any normal person would expect his or her bank to be able to tell them the exact amount in a current account, not everyone is ready to accept the quantification of concepts which are not customarily expressed in numerical units. Quite often the suspicion that is shown to quantitative data stems as much from a suspicion of what the measured units *mean* as from suspicion of the figures themselves.

It is therefore worth while considering why people wish to convey information in quantitative terms. One very simple reason is that certain forms of behaviour can only be performed if concepts are quantified. If a motorist exceeds the speed limit a court of law cannot judge from a police officer saying the driver was going 'very fast'. A tailor measuring a man for a made-to-measure suit cannot just list the man's dimensions as 'tall, portly with long legs and short arms'. Examples such as these may appear self-evident. But when librarians are faced with problems of proving their attempts to achieve economy, efficiency and effectiveness by the use of 'performance indicators' it is not as easy to recognize what to measure and how to measure it.

There are two main reasons for using quantitative measures, apart from the above needs for precise measurement. One is concerned with developments over time, or trends, and the other is concerned with making comparisons. Most chief librarians of public or academic libraries compile annual reports for the committees to whom they are responsible. The fact that annual reports are written derives from an assumption that something has happened during the past year and that developments of some sort have taken place. If the various activities that take place in the library can be quantified then it becomes possible to monitor the changes from year to year and to discern trends. Looking at the CIPFA Actuals for public libraries it is possible to see if accessions, stock or loans have increased or declined over a period of years. Expenditure on public libraries can be monitored from CIPFA statistics and on university libraries from UGC statistics. Having produced a set of figures for a trend over, say, five or ten years, or even more if standardized data are available, it is then possible to set trends against each other for comparison of one factor with another. Thus one could, for example, compare a ten-year trend of university library spending on books with spending on periodicals and both of these trends can be compared with the total funding received by the library, however defined.

But comparisons between trends are not the only comparisons for which quantitative data are useful. Individual libraries can gain valuable insights into their own performances, achievements and problems by comparing themselves with other libraries which they decide, on chosen criteria, are reasonably similar to themselves. Thus one county library authority may compare itself with another county of roughly similar resident population and discover that the one receives more money per 1000 population but spends less per 1000 population on books. Comparisons which are made by way of ratios, such as 'per 1000 population' help considerably in increasing the range of comparisons possible.

So far, then, we have established that quantitative methods have a great deal to offer librarians in increasing their understanding of their operations. Quantitative methods need not necessarily entail going out and doing surveys, since there are certain to be counts and measurements made of all sorts of aspects of a library's work as a normal part of the overall operation. What may be missing could be good, clean definitions of what is being counted, systematic ways of doing the counting and perception of what can be done with the figures once they have been collected. It can be surprising to see how little use is sometimes made of quantitative data that are routinely collected.

The Audit Commission has ruffled a few feathers by its work on trends, ratios and comparisons, work which could be carried out by anyone since the figures are usually quite accessible to the public. Critics of their work have claimed that the Audit Commission's calculations often show a lack of understanding of problems faced by the practising librarians, but the Audit Commission's figures most certainly do raise interesting questions for which it would often seem very reasonable to seek answers. The answers may well be descriptive, rather than quantitative, but this does not in itself invalidate the importance of the quantification in the first place.

3. What to quantify?
Some librarians must at times wonder why they collect statistics when the managerial or policy decisions seem to be made without reference to the statistics, or even prior to their collection. It must be accepted that committees do often ignore the objective information laid before them. This is a fact of life which must be accepted because policy is not infrequently based on prejudice, ideology or simple horse-trading. Committee members may not wish to be confused by considering facts if theories are to be implemented. But also experience shows that people who are quite literate are by no means always numerate and reports which contain tables of figures get scant attention. The first rule therefore in the collection and use of quantitative material is to keep it simple.

Social scientists who get carried away with their enthusiasm for quantitative data and development of formulae may well be doing important advanced work, but if their presentations are incomprehensible to those in authority they will get nowhere. It is not surprising that people welcome figures that support their own arguments and decry those that go against them. Any reading of Hansard will support this point. If the producer of the data is to convince sceptics or opponents then the figures must be easily understood and the connection between the data and the conclusions drawn from the data must be crystal clear.

Trying to keep quantitative data clear and understandable may not always be possible if the reasoning involved is unavoidably complicated, but researchers can help themselves if they take as the second rule to keep it understandable. Pie charts and histograms can be read more quickly than distribution frequencies and two places of decimals are not always necessary in a table. The important thing is to *use* the quantitative data to make or support an argument; readers are not entranced by the sheer weight of figures. In choosing what to quantify, therefore, the researcher should consider carefully what data are already available (or can easily be made available) and what data may have to be sought anew by going out and getting them.

For librarians, especially those with automated systems, it may be relatively simple to collect quite a lot of information about accessions, stock, reservations, overdues and possibly user behaviour (especially in academic libraries). Indeed, such is the versatility of the modern computer that it is only too easy to produce more information than one needs or can cope with. If one has a survey of, say, five activities of users analysed by five characteristics of those users the resultant print-out could be quite overpowering.

'What to quantify?' is best answered by a further question: 'What is it *for*?' Research data must be justified by their utility – they must say something that is relevant to the enquiry in hand and so a good question to ask is not: 'Is it interesting?' but: 'Is it relevant?', by which is meant that data collected must be worth having because they contribute something to the study in hand. It may be interesting to analyse an activity by the characteristic of sex, but unless there is some real point in knowing the differences between men and women in this activity the analysis is pointless. If, for example, one discovered that more men than women were fined for overdue books would this be of any value? If men were over-represented in those borrowers fined this could give rise to interesting hypotheses but unless the research was wanting to look directly at male/female differences this finding might well only complicate matters and would hardly suggest ways of improving library efficiency.

So perhaps the third rule should be to decide what you want to know and then go as directly as possible for the answers you need. Economy in research, even parsimony, is a desirable objective. Going ahead with unformulated objectives with a philosophy that something interesting is sure to turn up can be a recipe for disaster. A well designed research project works roughly along the following lines:

1. What is my problem? How do I define it?
2. How do I translate my problem into research work?

3. What data do I need to collect? What is relevant?
4. How do I analyse the data?
5. What will my analysis contribute to solving my problem?

As has already been pointed out, there may be data already accessible that can be adequate to meet the needs of 3. If, however, this is not the case then the researcher will have to think how the necessary data are to be collected.

4. Sources of data

Every research project has its unique problems and no guide to research can hope to deal with all of them. What can be said in general terms though is that all possible use should be made of quantitative data that are either already collected or which can be collected without much difficulty. In discussions of performance indicators the point is frequently made that libraries normally do collect quantitative data about certain aspects of their operations. Figures on income and expenditure, staffing and acquisitions, stock, loans and so on all tell interesting and useful stories. But it must be recognized that many of these measurements may have their limitations. For example, in the CIPFA Actuals a few library authorities return only one overall figure for their annual additions to lending book stock as they do not apparently keep separate records of their purchases of adult fiction, adult non-fiction and children's books. Although the purchase of paperback books is now very widespread, especially in public libraries, few authorities keep specific records of their accessions in hardback and paperback categories. When trying to relate expenditure on books to numbers of books bought, therefore, any average prices are greatly affected by the type of binding. Here, then, is an example of data which perhaps could be collected but rarely are because the management do not see any utility in their collection.

Most of the quantitative indicators mentioned above are input measures. Output measures are not as widespread, largely because they are not as simple to collect. Loans are, of course, a measure of output, but much of user behaviour cannot be recorded at an issue desk by means of automated processes and so researchers have to consider what they themselves can do to record systematically the characteristics, actions and perhaps attitudes of the people for whom the libraries are provided. If we call this phase of research 'observation' then it is possible to consider different sorts of observation that can lead up to formal surveys which provide quantitative data.

5. Observation

Data can be collected from two main sources – documents and observation; or put very simply from paper and people. We have already discussed how and why the researcher should make as much use as possible of documents that are available, especially when those documents contain quantitative material that helps to solve problems. But when documents are exhausted for their usefulness the researcher has to move on to collecting raw material from people themselves. What are the basic social characteristics of users? What do they do in the library? What are their opinions on key issues of library services? These are the general sorts of questions that library researchers need to have answered and which can only be answered by users themselves.

However, observation can be of many different sorts and before deciding to carry out a full-scale survey by means of interviews or self-completed questionnaires researchers should remember that a sample survey is the end product of a lot of preparatory work and will doubtless also involve a lot of work on analysis. A survey is not something to be undertaken lightly and at the drop of a hat. This chapter is not the one in which to consider all the different types of observation that can be used but the point must be made here that in most areas of social research it is possible to observe social behaviour through unobtrusive measures and with minimal participation.

Any library is a social setting where people's behaviour is, for the most part, reasonably open to view. So a library researcher wanting to study user behaviour would be very foolish to ignore the opportunities for simply watching what people do without letting the users know that they are being observed. This 'bird watching' technique can be most helpful at any early stage of survey work and there is no reason why it should not be done systematically. Thus the observer can easily monitor the sex of people entering the library and could make estimates of their age and social class. It may not be possible to follow round the library every person who enters it, but with sampling of entrants it is possible to record systematically what shelves people go to first, whether they seem purposive in their book selection or whether they appear to be browsing rather aimlessly, whether they begin their search of the A–Z author fiction at A or another letter, whether they seek only fiction, only non-fiction or both, and so on. Figure 4.1 shows a schedule that I used some years ago when my students at Sheffield University carried out systematic observations in the public library and in a bookshop. The results gave us some very useful descriptive insights into

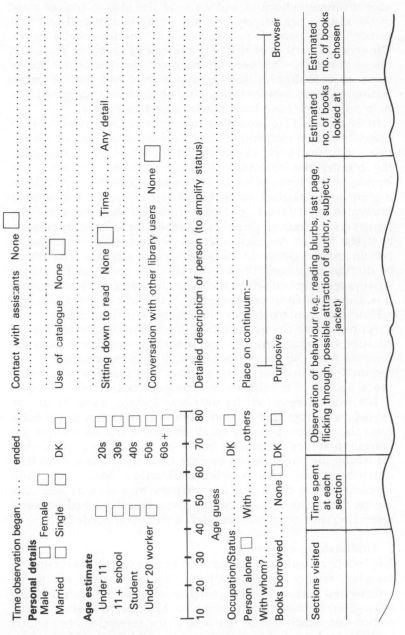

Fig. 4.1 Library schedule

user/customer behaviour and we were also able to analyse most of the data quantitatively because we agreed beforehand that certain items would be recorded in predetermined ways. Observation surveys of this sort also can be useful in recording things that do *not* happen; for example, very few of the library users or bookshop customers approached the staff of either institution for assistance though our observations suggested that help might well have been useful to certain people.

It is possible to combine unobtrusive observation with carefully chosen elements of deliberate intrusion by researchers. In a widespread survey I carried out of bookshops up and down the country the observers all asked assistants for advice on buying certain types of books – a cookery book being bought by a man, a car manual being bought by a woman and a book known to be definitely out of print by all the observers. The replies to the out of print query made for a most interesting analysis, but all the replies could be quantified according to certain analysis categories decided upon in advance. The asking of dummy questions of library staff has been carried out in surveys recently and whilst the descriptive analysis is interesting it is also possible to put percentages to some of the answers.

However, unobtrusive or minimally obtrusive measures as described above clearly have their limitations. These are mainly because the observers do not make any sustained personal contacts with the people observed. It may be instructive to a certain degree to observe that a library user makes a bee-line for the 's' section of the fiction-by-author shelves, but the observer is left wondering what the user was looking for if he or she moves away from that section without removing a single book from the shelves. I clearly recall observing two women in the bookshop survey examining books on football and wondering for whom they intended to buy the book they selected. To find out more about what people's total action means frequently requires asking them for the answers to questions and this means that some form of contact must be established between researcher and observed. In brief, a survey is needed.

6. Undertaking surveys

It is best to consider sample surveys of people initially according to whether the people involved, the informants, are to be interviewed personally by research workers or whether they are to be given (by carefully chosen means) a questionnaire for self-completion which will be returned to the researchers but which will not involve face-to-face questioning. Let us consider the pros and cons of these two main techniques, looking first at the use of the self-completed questionnaire since this may seem attractively easy.

Every ten years each household in this country is required to complete a questionnaire for the decennial census of population. Each year many people have to complete a questionnaire for the Inland Revenue. If you want to renew your passport or your car licence you expect to fill in a questionnaire. Government agencies have, in the past, been severely criticized for issuing very complicated questionnaires with inadequate instructions as to how to complete them. It is apparent today that much greater care is taken in compiling questionnaires and the accompanying instructions. However, recipients of census or income tax questionnaires have no choice about completing them and if we want a passport or car licence we must fill in the form (and pay the fee). Recently I received a questionnaire from the manufacturer of my two-year-old car asking for pages of answers to questions which would benefit them but did not seem to benefit me. I did reply, post-paid, but I did not answer many of the questions. I give this example because the researcher must ask himself very carefully in designing self-completion question- naires *why* should the respondent spend time filling it in? Response rate is very important for the success of any survey and a questionnaire that people will not answer can produce a worthless survey result. On the other hand an interview survey is likely to be an expensive business since labour costs will have to be paid for and unless the respondents are easily accessible it may simply be impossible to arrange interviews satisfactorily. For example, a systematic survey of the response of architects to criticisms of them made by the Prince of Wales would require interviews all over the country to get a proper sample, whereas a postal questionnaire could be on all their desks at more or less the same time.

Clearly the tactics of surveying need to be carefully considered before taking the plunge. Some years ago I was involved in pioneer work in surveys of theatre audiences. I had been given a grant to try to find out who goes to the theatre – in this instance the Sheffield Playhouse. I had about 20 questions I wanted answering and I had to think how best to achieve a good response. Interviewing members of the audience would be very difficult given the time available, the crush at any interval and the probable interference with people's night out. I then considered self-completion questionnaires on a sample basis but finally decided to try to survey the whole 'population', which could be 539 people at a full house. I designed a two-fold quarto size questionnaire printed on hard card with an appeal for help on the front cover and the questions on the two inside pages only. The back cover was left blank. For this survey the theatre programmes were single-stapled inside the questionnaires and everyone entering the auditorium was given the number of questionnaire/free programmes equal to their theatre tickets. Assistants with pencils roamed the aisles offering them to respondents and collecting completed questionnaires.

An appeal for completion was also broadcast before the curtain went up and boxes were provided for people to drop questionnaires in if the helpers missed them. Two runs of plays of three weeks' duration were surveyed in all, with a one-night pilot survey of a previous production to test out the technique. The pilot survey attained a response rate of 96.4% and the two three-week runs produced response rates of 91.9% and 92.5% of audiences, with a range from 84.3% to 98.4% for evening performances (one poorly attended and not well administered matinee hit a nadir of 77.0%). This technique was subsequently used for surveys of drama, ballet and opera at the Grand Theatre, Leeds, and for surveys of orchestral concerts in England and Scotland. Subsequent experience showed that it was not necessary to incorporate give-away programmes with the questionnaires.

This example is not directly relevant to library surveys since the users of libraries are not like the captive audience (pardon the pun) that one has in a theatre. But the example does, I hope, illustrate that the survey researcher should always look for a technique that is appropriate to the problem in hand. For example, perhaps a survey of student users might be better carried out in the lecture room rather than the library itself if particular groups of students are the target. Horses for courses is a good guide for carrying out surveys and researchers should not allow themselves to be conventional if the unconventional pays off better.

7. Questionnaires and interview schedules
Whilst both self-completed questionnaires and interview schedules filled in by interviewers themselves have a lot in common, particularly in their construction, it is necessary to be quite clear about the desirability of these survey instruments for any particular job in hand. Let us begin by considering in detail the utility and restrictions of the self-completed questionnaire.

Firstly, it seems attractive because the respondents will do most of the work for you; they will both read the questions and enter the answers. Where personal interviews may be impossible, perhaps because of scatter of informants or because their numbers are too much to cope with by interview, then the questionnaire has its attractions. But the compiler of any such questionnaire must give considerable thought to its design because the printed page has to do all the introductory and subsequent work that an interviewer would do by speech. Thus, the postal questionnaire, for example, has to introduce itself by means of a written appeal for help which will convince the recipient that here is a survey that is worth participating in to begin with and here is a set of questions that he or she can and will answer. The researcher should, therefore, ask himself what sort of information he is looking for in the survey and how likely he is to obtain that information from the respondents in his sample, whatever type of people they may be.

One fundamental error made by too many questionnaire compilers is to allow the questionnaire to become too long and involved. In interviews the respondents cannot be sure what is coming and how long it will take, but the recipient of a 15-page questionnaire knows at once what lies in store – and may well opt out.

Questionnaires sometimes become too complicated because the researchers are seeking too much depth in the questions. In interviews it is not difficult to follow up alternative lines of probing from an initial starter question, but if this is attempted on paper the result can be most off-putting to the recipient. Self-completed questionnaires are, in general, better for breadth than depth and if there are too many tricky questions to deal with respondents may become confused, suspicious or even bored and all these factors can reduce the response rate.

As well as thinking carefully about the questions in a self-completed questionnaire it is vitally important to think also about the possible answers. All survey design requires the researcher to think a lot about how to help the respondent. In designing a self-completed questionnaire the researcher must forever be trying to think how this question and that answer can be made easier for the respondent. One very obvious way of helping is to provide boxes for the respondent to tick in according to how he or she selects certain predetermined answers. At the most basic level personal details such as sex, age group and marital status can be dealt with by pre-set answers with boxes to tick in, all of which makes it simpler and quicker for the respondent and also makes subsequent analysis easier for the researcher. However, pre-set answers require thought because they must be comprehensive and comprehensible. Marital status was easier to categorize when one could be fairly sure that almost everyone was single, married, widowed or divorced. Then with increasing divorce rates a further category of 'separated' became useful for certain surveys. Nowadays with so many unmarried people living together in stable relationships, sometimes with children, it is necessary to try to add yet another category which covers cohabitation without seeming to pass a moral judgement – for example, 'living in sin' is not a recommended term to use.

There is a certain amount of debate about whether respondents to self-completed questionnaires are more or less likely to give very personal details about themselves compared with what they would say to an interviewer. It is very difficult to generalize on this matter since every survey is different, but certainly people are much franker today about their private lives than they used to be, though they may still find it easier to give information about personal details by speech rather than writing it down. Thus a respondent might acknowledge, during an interview, that he or she has in the past stolen a book from a library, but faced with the written question: 'Have you ever stolen a book from your local public library?', the same respondent could well not be prepared to commit the answer to paper. Experienced interviewers can develop a line of questioning so that it becomes an interesting conversation and it can be quite surprising how much interviewed people will tell complete strangers. Self-completed questionnaires can never develop this personal rapport.

8. Respondents

Postal questionnaires work best when the researcher can be fairly sure that the recipients already have an interest in the topic being researched and can see the point of the survey itself. If the completed survey report will result in a useful feed-back to the contributors then there is a good reason for spending time and effort on completing the questionnaire. It therefore follows that postal questionnaires are most suitable for people who already have a bond of common interest and who can be expected to be benevolently disposed to giving details of their actions, opinions and personal data. I have myself carried out several large scale postal surveys of members of the National Trust, asking questions about members' interests, activities and opinions of current matters being dealt with by the Trust. The response rates have always been good (if at times rather slow) because the respondents could feel that their replies were helping their organization to do a better job. By contrast, when I surveyed visitors to the British Museum some years ago I would not have contemplated handing out self-completion questionnaires to be posted back to me. Such informants have to be 'caught' there and then by interviewers to achieve a good response. People visiting museums and such places may have a common interest (though so many at the British Museum were overseas tourists that this common interest was often little more than sight-seeing) but they will not necessarily feel a common bond between themselves, nor will they feel any particular bond with the institution carrying out the survey. When I surveyed the Sheffield Playhouse in the 1960s nearly 40% of the audience then had regular bookings and there was a strong local feeling of support by attenders for 'their' theatre. Hence the audience questionnaire method was less of a gamble than it might have seemed at first. In the surveys of drama, opera and orchestral concerts it was possible to use the Arts Council support as a peg to hang the appeal on, as well as the hope in Leeds that the survey might result in more tours by the so-called national companies usually resident in London.

9. The appeal

I have already mentioned above that, to achieve a good response in a survey, the researcher must give careful thought to the problem of making an appeal to respondents to help. When street interviewers do surveys they have to make their appeal very quickly and very succinctly and it is sometimes surprising how kind the great British public is to interviewers who interrupt their shopping expeditions with questions about double glazing or other such less than earth-shattering topics. All my experience of library surveys indicates that library users tend to be helpful informants who can usually be expected to agree to be interviewed unless they are in a hurry to get away. Certainly if the appeal to them is to help improve library services then the self-interest of the respondent can be utilized at once.

But where there is no smiling, kindly interviewer and the appeal must be made in writing things can be much more difficult. Any postal or unaccompanied questionnaire should have with it a not-too-long appeal for help which will instantly make clear what this is all about. The letter (which the appeal actually is) must explain the purpose of the survey and make it seem interesting and relevant to the recipient. It should try to deal in advance quite positively with any queries or quibbles the recipient might have and it must be absolutely clear who is carrying out the survey. In most surveys the replies are of no less value if they are anonymous so it is often possible to assure respondents that their replies will be destroyed after analysis, though this should always be done in a way that does not suggest the document could be in any way damaging to the respondent.

If one tries to put oneself in the shoes of the respondent who opens an envelope containing a completely unsolicited questionnaire it is not too difficult to anticipate a few questions that are likely to arise, which the appeal should deal with at once, so as to get the respondent involved and ready to do the work of completion. From the point of view of the respondent then:

1. Where has this questionnaire come from? Who is doing this survey? Headed notepaper and an actual signature of the researcher should make it clear that this is no hole-and-corner affair and that it is not a covered-up sales campaign.

2. Why should I, personally, fill in this questionnaire? Here the appeal must suggest that the individual respondent will be helping a larger group, an organization or a particular activity by making his or her own contribution. The larger 'cause' must be clear.

3. Will I be able to fill in this questionnaire? It is off-putting and even annoying to recipients to be presented with questions that are impossible for them to answer, or which require a great deal of work to be done in compiling an answer. Questions such as: 'How many books have you borrowed over the past six months?' or: 'How often have you been fined for overdue books in the past five years?' may seem innocuous to the question asker but may well infuriate the respondent who has no idea and no means (or intention) of finding out.

10. Facilitating replies

Amongst the many things a researcher has to consider when sending out a postal questionnaire is how best to get the questionnaires back again in large numbers. Any questionnaire which is not accompanied by a self-addressed envelope, post paid where appropriate, does not deserve to be returned. In some cases where the questionnaire covers only one side of A4 it is possible to print the reply address on the other side, with the appropriate pre-paid postage markings, but let us consider the questionnaire with envelope. If the questionnaire itself, with its accompanying letter of appeal, is not too bulky it can be folded once across the middle and sent in a 24 × 16 cm envelope. The return envelope can then either be another envelope of the same size folded in half or perhaps a 23 × 10 cm envelope unfolded if the questionnaire is not too bulky. Whatever reply envelope is used the return name and address should be quite clear, peel-off labels being usually adequate. If the research organization conducting the survey is involved in regular surveys it is well worth arranging with the Post Office for either a business reply licence or a Freepost facility. In both cases a small extra charge is levied for each envelope returned, but there is no charge for the non-response.

If, however, the survey is not to make use of such pre-paid facilities then a postage stamp should be stuck on the reply envelope since it is quite wrong to expect any respondent to pay postage. Surveys going to people overseas can create problems; postage vouchers can be used, though they are clearly less satisfactory. When stamps are used in the UK there is always a possibility of recipients steaming them off, but this is a hazard that must be accepted. I once did a survey of 986 students at Sheffield University, studying their use of books. As a member of staff I could have distributed the questionnaires via the university's internal postal system at virtually no cost and students could have dropped their replies off at the main porters' lodge. However, I felt that I wanted my approach to each student to be as personal as possible, so I posted every questionnaire to each student at his or her term-time address and I sent a stamped addressed envelope for the reply. A few enterprising students did steam off the stamps and leave their replies at the porters' lodge but most came back to me via the Post Office. I cannot claim that this mode of delivery and return increased the response rate, since I had no control group for comparison, but the response rate was 77%, which I considered good for a sample of this kind.

When a survey is mailed out it is always interesting, as well as essential, to monitor the rate of response. There are always the few replies that seem to be returned almost before the letters have been posted but usually there is a pattern of increasing numbers coming back until a peak, or even a plateau, is reached. After that there is a decline in the rate of reply and the researcher must take a decision about sending out a follow-up letter. The wording of this must be very delicate since one is really prodding people to get a move on. Tactics will vary according to circumstances with each survey, but one can consider sending a second questionnaire with a letter suggesting that perhaps the first one never reached the respondent. One can also make the point that it is not too late to reply and that a high response rate *is* important. Whatever wording is chosen the writer must not bully or demand. Filling in survey questionnaires is almost always voluntary and no researcher should ever be rude to a respondent.

In most cases of general surveys I think that the one follow-up letter is as much as one should venture upon, since a second request can irritate and may well not produce anything anyway. But sometimes one is involved in special surveys of groups where a 100% response is really to be sought. In such an instance I favour the telephone call to the person addressed with a gentle verbal request. Actually, in some special surveys involving senior librarians I find that speaking to the librarian's secretary is the most productive method of all – one learns who really runs the office!

I suggested earlier in this chapter that postal or other similar surveys using self-completed questionnaires can suffer from low response rates and that interview surveys can often achieve better responses. Yet my own theatre audience surveys achieved some of the highest response rates I have ever had, so there are no absolute certainties in survey work. Nevertheless, surveys conducted by personal interviews do have advantages which occur from there being personal contact between the interviewer and interviewed. It is a point that when a research worker approaches an informant asking if he or she can spare a few minutes to be interviewed about 'X' the respondent has to say 'no' to get out of it – and a surprising number of people seem reluctant to do so.

This does not mean, though, that interviewers can count on a welcome from every potential respondent they approach. Interviewers need to be properly trained about the general approach to be used and the specific explanation for the particular survey. Interviewers, especially those who do house-to-house or street interviews, also need today to carry proper identification cards or documents to establish their bona fides if challenged. I also find that when interviewing in institutions such as museums, stately homes and libraries that a simple badge saying 'SURVEY' seems to reassure people that the interviewer is somehow official.

Interview surveys in the street or in premises such as libraries present problems of sampling which are not the concern of this chapter, but it must be obvious that every refusal to be interviewed dilutes the sample, even if substitutes are used. Street interviewing presents many problems of deciding where to station the interviewers, what time of day to survey and what to do when it pours with rain. House-to-house surveying can present problems of finding people at home and institutional surveying, as in libraries, can be beset by problems of getting people to give of their time if the survey is done, as is commonplace, at the end of the visit. When I had five inter-viewers working simultaneously on the British Museum survey I arranged for them to have tables in the entrance halls where informants could be interviewed whilst seated. It was interesting to see how welcome the sit-down was to many visitors who had just completed a long walk round the exhibits. It also meant that once an informant had sat down he or she was virtually committed to the full interview.

In general, therefore, one can conclude this section by saying that satisfactory quantitative data obtained through surveys depends on the researcher giving very careful thought to anything and everything that can be done to achieve a high response rate. Surveying is anything but a mechanical process if people think hard about what they are doing.

Further reading

Gardner, G., *Social surveys for social planners*, Milton Keynes, The Open University Press, 1978.

Hoinville, G., *et al.*, *Survey research practice*, London, Heine-mann, 1978.

Line, M. B., *Library surveys* (2nd edition, edited by S. Stone), London, Bingley, 1982.

Mann, P. H., *Methods of social investigation*, Oxford, Blackwell, 1985.

Runcie, J. F., *Experiencing social research*, Homewood, Illinois, The Dorsey Press, 1976.

5 Asking questions: Questionnaire design and question phrasing

Paul Burton

1. Asking questions

Asking questions in the form of questionnaires ranks as one of the most popular research methods, and there are a number of reasons why this is so. They are often a convenient way to obtain data from a large population or sample, particularly if the population is geographically dispersed and travel is not feasible for one reason or another. Properly constructed, a questionnaire can also elicit a great deal of information on the survey topic, particularly if quantitative data only are sought, and the relative costs of the survey are reduced. Many would suggest that because the questionnaire is more anonymous than the interview, respondents are likely to be more candid. Similarly, the personal influence of the interviewer is avoided: sex, ethnic origin and perceived social status may all influence the accuracy of the interview, but can be eliminated in the questionnaire.

For these reasons, it seems a simple matter to decide to 'send out a questionnaire', and certainly numerous questionnaires of varying quality appear in the librarian's mail tray. However, to obtain accurate and worthwhile results requires careful preparation and testing. Without this preparation, it is too easy to introduce bias into questions or to frame questions which cannot be answered by the respondent or analysed by the researcher.

Questionnaires have further disadvantages inherent in their nature. Response rates often tend to be low, even if a reply envelope is provided: the questionnaire is put aside for answering in the near future, and is then forgotten or completed too late. There is, after all, little apparent incentive to complete a questionnaire. A commonly asked question is 'what constitutes an acceptable response rate for questionnaires?', but is not an easy one to answer. Generally, experience suggests that 60% or more is very acceptable. Assuming that the sample has been properly drawn, anything less than 50% represents a minority, and in some cases this will effectively render the results of little or no practical value. However, it can be argued that even a response rate of less than 50% tells the researcher *something* about the problem under study: a slight trend may be detectable, a grouping of attitudes may be evident, etc. There is always the danger that what response there is comes from an unrepresentative portion of the population (some people really like to complete questionnaires!), but provided that the low response rate is clearly borne in mind, it might then be more profitable to revise the survey by concentrating on what trends or patterns have been detected and endeavour to find out more about them.

Reading disabilities among the population will clearly influence the effectiveness of the survey, as will visual handicap, while some respondents may complete the questionnaire in a confusing way, either because they have failed to understand how to complete it (a fault of the researcher, not the respondent) or have not paid enough attention to the questions. (A common problem is to find each of two alternatives ticked or circled: presumably one has been marked in error – but which one?) In cases such as this, there is rarely an opportunity to seek clarification, which would be possible in an interview.

Questionnaires frequently seek quantitative information, and this tends to make them easier to complete, but it is perfectly possible to seek more qualitative data in this way by using open ended questions. These, however, are more difficult to analyse, a factor discussed below.

2. Clarity and precision of questions
Simply writing down a list of apparently relevant questions does not constitute designing an effective questionnaire. The researcher must have a clear definition of the objectives of the research before being able to ask the appropriate questions. Stating the objective as, for example, 'to study library users' is too vague: it begs the question 'who is a library user?', what constitutes library use, and so on.

Once the objective of the survey has been established, it is possible to determine the questions which will elicit the required information. Every effort should be made to avoid asking questions which are not strictly relevant to the objectives of the survey. It can be easy to add questions because 'it might be nice to know about X' when, in fact, X will play no part in the study, and respondents will be quick to take exception to irrelevancies, with consequent effects on response rate.

It is here too that *terminology and jargon* will pose a problem, though much will depend on the survey population. Questionnaires aimed at professional library staff can usually employ accepted terminology, of course, though clarification may be required for newer terms (buzzwords) or for terms used in a particular way by the researcher (for example, does 'information technology' include smart telephone exchanges and intelligent photocopiers?). However, even with a professional population, ambiguity may result, requiring further definition or clarification. What, for example, may be meant by the term 'periodical'? Does it, for the purposes of the questionnaire, extend to annual publications, or are these to be counted as monographs? What is report literature?

Terminology and jargon (or their lack) play a major role in obtaining accurate responses from a general user population. For the researcher immersed in the subject matter, it is too easy to forget that the target population may not understand terms used or may have a different understanding. Many library users, for example, refer to the catalogue as the 'library index': if questions are also asked about indexing journals, confusion will abound! How many users would understand the term OPAC, even when it is spelled out?

An effective way to ensure that terminology is clear and unambiguous and that questions are relevant to the purposes of the research is to pre-test or pilot the questionnaire.

Problems of clarity and precision remain, however, even when jargon is defined. If we return to the example of 'studying library users', we said that this failed to define the user and use. User could be extended to include all those who come into the library on a specific day or days as Peter Mann suggested in the last chapter, but it could equally be defined as registered members of the library. Use of a library ranges from asking a simple question in the reference section to exploiting its resources in order to write an academic paper. Imprecise questions such as those about use must make clear what is meant, and there are basically two ways in which this clarification can be obtained.

Questions can be *open-ended* (with some suggested answers) to be completed by the respondent in his or her own words. It might, however, be easier to provide the user with *closed questions*, providing a list of potential reasons for visiting the library, for example, and ask him or her to tick one (if the object of the study is to establish the main purpose of the visit) or as many as are applicable (if all reasons are sought). This pre-supposes, of course, that the researcher is familiar enough with potential reasons for using a library to draw up such a list. The relative merits of open and closed questions are discussed below.

Ambiguity in questions may be difficult to eliminate, simply because the researcher fails to see any ambiguity (another reason for piloting the study first). On occasion, the context of the questionnaire will remove any ambiguities, since the particular term will be seen in the light of previous questions, but this may not always be the case, and in general it is desirable not to rely on the context as a means to clarification. We have already seen how certain technical terms (such as 'catalogue') may be misinterpreted, but these are not the sole source of ambiguity.

Questions may often be asked to establish the frequency of an event, in which the respondent is asked to select from a list of possible answers. Terms such as 'often', 'occasionally', or 'frequently' should be avoided, as each respondent will have a different understanding of what these can mean. Frequent use of indexing and abstracting journals may mean once a week to some (which would be both frequent and regular), and on every library visit to others. Similar remarks will apply to comparable questions such as: 'How do you evaluate the interlibrary loan service: good, fair, or poor?', since these are relative terms which will differ for each respondent.

Questions relating to the frequency of events should be provided with specific intervals appropriate to the topic. Thus, a question on use of abstracting and indexing journals could be phrased:

Approximately how often do you use the abstracting and indexing journals?
Once per week   . . . .
Once per fortnight   . . . .
Once per month   . . . .
Less frequently   . . . .
Never   . . . .

Evaluative questions are perhaps less easy to construct, but can be done with the use of numbered scales or carefully chosen statements with which the respondent expresses some level of agreement.

Both types of question should contain an odd number of scale points or statements, so that a mid-point can be set which will normally allow for a neutral response such as 'Don't know' or 'Neither agree nor disagree'. Without such a mid-point, respondents may be forced to select an option which does not truly reflect their views or will ignore the question which could distort results. Typical scale points are 1 to 3, 1 to 5 and 1 to 7, though three points might not provide an adequate spread of options, while seven might mean (for verbal expressions) that the divisions are too small. Five points are usually sufficient for scales with verbal expressions, though numeric scales would normally have seven gradations.

Typical numerical scale questions can be constructed on the following lines:

On a scale of 1 to 7 (when 1 = good and 7 = poor), how would you rate the library's provision of abstracting and indexing tools?

It is also possible, and often desirable, to combine a number of related questions with numerical scales, so that a set of responses is gathered in one question. Thus, the last example could be one of a set on the library's provision of various reference tools taking the following form:

On a scale of 1 to 7 (1 = good and 7 = poor), how would you rate the library's provision of the following reference tools?
(Please circle one number for each category)

Abstracting and indexing periodicals	1 2 3 4 5 6 7
Encyclopedias	1 2 3 4 5 6 7
Bibliographies	1 2 3 4 5 6 7
Dictionaries	1 2 3 4 5 6 7

Again with the assumption that all the 'technical' terms in this question had been clearly defined, scaled questions such as these will remove much of the ambiguity inherent in evaluations.

Scaling is also possible with non-numeric responses (verbal expressions) which again will range from one extreme to the other. Here, as suggested, five gradations are normally sufficient to provide a suitable range. Using verbal expressions, the numeric example above would appear as:

Please indicate how adequate you feel the library's provision of the following reference tools to be. (Please tick one answer for each category.)

	Seriously inadequate	Inadequate	Adequate	More than adequate	Good
Abstracting and index-ing period-icals					
Encyclopedias					
Bibliographies					
Dictionaries					

Note the slightly different wording in this question, which is to emphasize that it is the respondent's own evaluation which is sought and not some generalized idea.

A variation on the verbal expression scale may be used to elicit the extent of agreement with various statements. Again, it is normal practice to have a range of five answers, from positive to negative, with a neutral mid-point.

Figure 5.1 provides an example of a further range of questions about reference works which could expand on users' views on this aspect of the service. Notice that, in figure 5.1, both positive and negative statements have been included. This is not an attempt to be negative, but a technique which helps to ensure that respondents read and think about the question, rather than slip into a pattern of automatic agreement or disagreement. This is also easy to do with scalar questions which are always presented in the same order (i.e. negative or positive aspect first). There is some disagreement in the literature on this question of always presenting the same aspect at the same end of the scale (e.g., positive always on the left), but in general it is a good idea to change the order from time to time. The order and arrangement of questions is discussed in more detail below.

Rating scales also demonstrate another method by which questionnaires may be used to elicit qualitative, rather than quantitative, data.

Scales such as those in the examples can be constructed and analysed with some ease (but also some thought), but there are more sophisticated techniques in the researcher's armoury, particularly when asking a number of questions on the same topic. One of the most popular of these techniques is the Likert scale, which, unlike Thurstone scales or Guttman's Scalogram, involves less effort in calculation. It is not possible to go into the details of Likert scales here, but essentially the procedure involves allocating scores to statements for which the respond-

	Strongly agree	Agree	Neither agree nor disagree	Disagree	Strongly disagree
Library reference works are adequate for my purposes					
Bibliographies are too out of date for my needs					
Abstracting and indexing journals are up to date					
Abstracting and indexing journals are difficult to use well					
Dictionaries serve little purpose in my work					
Encyclopedias contain enough information for my needs					

Fig. 5.1 Verbal expression scale

ents can select a range of responses from 'strongly agree' to 'strongly disagree'. The procedure is particularly useful in selecting the best statements for the final version of the questionnaire. (These techniques are discussed in the items in the bibliography.)

Clarity and precision in a questionnaire can also be affected by bias, the use of double negatives and double questions, hypothetical statements or questions, and assumptions, all of which should be avoided because they will also distort responses and thus the findings of the survey.

Bias and loaded questions are not always easy to detect, particularly by the researcher, who is usually too close to the subject, and this, therefore, is another reason for ensuring that questionnaires are pre-tested and piloted first. It is astonishing how many surveys are reported in the press which 'prove' a certain point which turns out to be the main platform of the organization commissioning the survey! Loading of questions can be brought about by something as apparently innocent as beginning a question with: 'In general, the majority of people feel that .... Do you agree?', which puts pressure on the respondent to go along with the majority view. Highly controversial subjects such as pornography or charging for library services, and politically- or ideologically-oriented questions relating, for example, to local authority provision of services, are easily loaded. Having the questionnaire pre-tested by both opponents and supporters of the topic in question will ensure that bias is removed.

Loading and the associated problems of *unspoken assumptions* can, however, be more subtle. A survey on library use, for example, could begin with the question: 'How often do you use the library?', but this clearly makes an assumption about the respondent's behaviour – that he or she does in fact use the library – and the respondent may well feel the need to reply positively. To avoid this assumption, it is necessary first to establish whether in fact the respondent does engage in the particular activity and then to establish the frequency, etc. Thus, our question must be preceded by: 'Do you use the library?' (YES/NO), or be re-phrased to provide a range of alternatives about frequency of use which includes a 'Never' option. Without this option, the respondent may feel obliged to answer with some level of frequency in order to conform with the unspoken assumption that he *should* use the library. As a leading question, it is therefore related to the pressure of the majority view mentioned above.

The danger in the use of *double negatives* lies mainly in the confusion they can cause in the respondent's mind and thus the risk in obtaining an incorrect answer. Consider, as an example, the question:

Charges for library services should not be introduced for basic services.
Agree .... Disagree .... Neither agree nor disagree ....

It requires some thought to appreciate just what is meant by disagreeing with this statement, and it is possible to find more complicated examples. This should not, however, be confused with the use of negative questions considered earlier, in which comprehension is easier to achieve. Simply avoiding the use of the word 'not' is usually sufficient.

Double questions (two questions in one) can also affect precision, since respondents may be able to agree with one part but not the other. An extreme example is:

Charges for library services should be introduced, but should be for additional services only.

(This assumes a definition of charges and additional services.) The question as presented does not allow an answer for the respondent who is opposed to library charges *in toto*, and has to be presented as two separate questions.

As is so often the case, *hypothetical questions* merely elicit hypothetical answers, the validity of which is questionable. At best, the answer to a question such as:

If charges for library services were introduced, do you think that your use of the service would
Increase   . . . .
Decrease   . . . .
Remain the same   . . . .?

could only be seen in the analysis as having minor predictive power, since the specific effects on use could be affected by many other factors. However, this is not to deny that hypothetical questions have a value, merely to emphasize that they must always be seen as hypothetical and not as firm statements of intent from respondents. They may, however, contain valuable indicators of future areas of research.

3. Questionnaire construction

Once the questions to be posed have been determined, the researcher must also consider the structure of the questions themselves. Questions can be *closed* or *open-ended*, and closed questions may require one or a number of options to be selected as responses. Both types of question can be used to elicit facts or opinions, but which should be adopted will depend on various factors (which are discussed below), on the general approach to the survey and on the analysis which can be carried out.

Many questionnaire surveys seek to establish quantitative data on the research topic and so, not surprisingly, the questions are almost entirely factual. In such cases, closed questions will predominate, though the provision of an 'Other' category may often elicit responses which are less easy to categorize. Quantitative data are generally easier to analyse, particularly with computer assistance. However, qualitative data can also be obtained through questionnaires, not least with open-ended questions: the analysis is less easy and usually less amenable to computer techniques.

It is not recommended, however, that the questionnaire be constructed with the specific aim of asking only closed or only open-ended questions, since this will place too great a constraint on the research. The research topic, and thus the questions it engenders, must be allowed to determine which questions are asked and how, though it cannot be denied that the resources available for analysis will also be a determining factor.

Closed questions are of two types, single choice or multiple choice: the most significant factor is that closed questions provide a limited (in relative terms) set of options from which the respondent must choose. Single choice questions require the respondent to select only one answer from the two or more provided and so are obviously only suitable when the responses available are mutually exclusive, and care must be taken to ensure that this is the case. Typical questions in this category relate to the age or sex of the respondent, the department or group to which he or she belongs (e.g. staff, student, postgraduate research), and so on. It is possible to make a set of options mutually exclusive by the use in the question of such qualifiers as 'Which of the following is your *main* area of interest' or 'What is your *principal* use of the service', but these should be used with care (if at all), since the respondent may not always be able to make such a distinction, and to do so will force an inaccurate response. A lecturer may visit the library to return or renew books, check for the availability of references, consult the latest issue of a journal and check recent issues of a published index for any publications in his field: he may regard none of these as the principal reason for his visit.

By contrast, closed questions which are not mutually exclusive allow the respondent to select each of the responses which apply.

Inaccurate responses to closed questions may come from a list of options which is not sufficiently comprehensive. The respondent may then be forced to select the response which is closest to his or her own situation, but which is not accurate. To ensure that the possible options are as complete as possible requires a background knowledge of the research topic and pre-testing, which will highlight any missing options. The situation can be helped by the provision of an 'Other' category, which will allow the respondent to add any category not listed. At the pre-testing stage, it will be evident if the list of categories is not sufficiently large when there are too many 'others', and these should be examined to determine what additional categories they contain which should, therefore, be included in the final version.

It should go without saying that, if respondents are expected to select one or a number from a list of options, this fact should be clearly indicated. An example of both types of closed question is given in Figure 5.2. Note the instructions, the use of an 'other' category with the request to be specific, and the fact that respondents are required to answer 'yes' or 'no', rather than simply tick the relevant answers. Without this approach, there is a danger that a response may be missed out by the respondent and subsequently read, during the analysis, as a service not used.

Open-ended questions do not provide a set list of responses, but allow the respondent to answer in his or her own words. Depending on the questions, this means that sufficient space for an adequate answer must be left (the answer may otherwise be reduced to what will fit), and such questions are less easy to analyse afterwards. Open-ended questions allow the respondent to provide a full answer (not one limited to the options supplied by the researcher) and can be a fruitful source of quotations which will 'flesh out' the final report. However, they are difficult to analyse, not least because respondents will almost certainly use different terms for the same thing (or it may be difficult to determine whether in fact they are saying the same thing), and the additional effort required to answer them may result in distortion of the respondent's real attitude.

Q1 Are you (tick one):
A member of university lecturing staff?   . . . .
A member of university administrative staff?   . . . .
An undergraduate student?   . . . .
A postgraduate student on a taught course?   . . . .
A postgraduate research student?   . . . .
Other (please specify)   . . . .

Q2 What is the purpose of your visit to the library today? (Tick any that apply.)   Yes   No
Return books   . . . .
Renew books   . . . .
Consult journals   . . . .
Consult bibliographies   . . . .
Trace references   . . . .
Read newspapers   . . . .
Browse among new books   . . . .
To write   . . . .
To study   . . . .
Other purpose (please specify)   . . . .

Fig. 5.2 Closed questions

The analysis of open questions, though problematic, is not impossible. The responses must be studied with care to isolate answers with elements in common into a coding frame for further analysis: this is a time-consuming task, and there is always the risk that the researcher 'forces' an answer into an inappropriate frame for neatness or convenience.

Despite these problems, open-ended questions should not be avoided, particularly when opinions and attitudes are sought by the research. They are valuable in the early phases of research, when they may provide the basis for subsequent closed questions, and provide much more detailed data (subject to an ability to analyse them).

A potentially useful form of question which can combine open-ended and closed questions is the 'critical incident', in which the respondent is asked to provide details of the last time he or she carried out a relevant action or thought about a relevant problem. Thus, a typical closed question is:

> Please think back to the last time you visited the library. On that occasion, which of the following services did you use? (Please tick all that apply.)

The critical incident question has the advantage of focusing the respondent's mind and of providing data on a specific occurrence. However, it does rely entirely on the accuracy of the respondent's memory, and if a previous question has established that (in this example) the last use of the library was some considerable time ago, the answers must be treated with caution. It must also be borne in mind that the last time may not have been typical (though this could be established with a supplementary question).

4. Structure and layout of questionnaires

By this we mean the layout of the questionnaire and the order of questions within it. Both are important in ensuring that the questionnaire is easy to complete, but is completed correctly and accurately, without any undue influence on the responses.

Questionnaires should start with the more general (but still relevant) questions, which have the effect of putting the respondent at ease. It is good practice to explain why personal questions (age, sex, marital status, income, etc.) are being asked, particularly if there is a chance that the respondent might feel they are irrelevant to the study.

Proceeding from the general to the specific helps to set the context of the enquiry, ensures proper understanding of the questions, and is also the most logical order in most cases, though some topics may have their own internal order which should be followed. A logical order (determined by the survey topic) should always be adhered to, and questions relating to the same topic should be grouped together, with subdivisions as appropriate. Beginning each group with a statement such as 'Questions 1 to 6 deal with charges for library services' helps to focus the respondent on that topic.

In certain cases, the answer to one question will determine which subsequent questions are to be answered, and in these cases certain intermediate questions will be irrelevant. For example, if the respondent answers 'no' to the question 'Have you ever used the Science Citation Index?', there is little point in then asking questions about how easy it was to use! In this case, it will be necessary to include instructions to the non-user as to which question he should now go to, and these must be clear and, of course, accurate, ensuring that other relevant questions are not missed. The instructions can be given as commands such as 'Please go to Q8' (placed beside the relevant answer) or with arrows to the next relevant question. (A good example of this last practice is on the application form for a UK passport.) Once again, pre-testing will show if instructions are clear and accurate, and it is a good idea to draw up a flow chart of the questionnaire to ensure that questions are not missed.

Consistency of format is also important. Always choose one method of answering and stick with it throughout the questionnaire. Closed questions can be provided with boxes, lines, or numbers, and these can be ticked or circled. Select one of these and use it throughout.

5. Piloting the questionnaire

Piloting a questionnaire normally involves drafting a version in the proposed order and discussing it with colleagues in the survey (if there are any) or with others, some of whom should have no knowledge of the background to the study. This will remove any immediate problems of clarity, understanding (particularly of jargon and 'professional' terminology), order of questions, etc., but this revised version should also be piloted with a small sample of the population for whom the questionnaire is designed. Ideally, this should include some mechanism for feedback from respondents and this could be done by having them complete a final question on how easy they found it to complete the questionnaire or by interviewing them as soon as possible after completion. The process must continue until the questionnaire is deemed suitable for the objectives of the research. It may therefore go through a number of iterations, but this is a necessary part of questionnaire design.

6. Providing the background to the research

Providing details of the research will always help the respondent to set the questionnaire in context, focus his or her mind on the specific problem and helps to justify the effort which will have to be expended on completing the questionnaire. This can best be done in a covering letter sent with the questionnaire. In addition, a covering letter will establish the researcher's credentials for carrying out the survey.

The covering letter, therefore, should explain who the researcher is, and who (if anyone) is sponsoring or funding the research. The purposes of the research should be set out clearly but concisely, together with a statement of the anticipated value of the study and why a questionnaire has been addressed to the respondent. In addition, it is important to tell respondents what use will be made of the results: it may be intended to publish the results, pass them to the funding organization or some other body, or use them in a further piece of research. All of this must be explained so that respondents know precisely what will happen to their answers.

It is normal to guarantee confidentiality and to emphasize that respondents will not be identifiable as individuals and it must be evident that this is so. Unless some sort of follow-up is intended (e.g. by an interview), it will not be necessary to ask for a name, but questionnaires will normally be numbered for administrative convenience and some respondents may suspect that this will be used to identify them. Assure them that this is not the case by explaining what the numbering means.

For postal questionnaires, include a stamped addressed envelope for the reply. At the design stage, a policy on sending out reminders should have been determined, and so return date should be specified. Reminders to those who have not returned the questionnaire by that date can be sent out after a suitable interval (usually three or four weeks), together with a second copy of the questionnaire and another return envelope.

7. Conclusion

Properly designed and analysed, questionnaires can be a rich and reliable source of research data, both quantitative and qualitative. Carrying out a questionnaire survey is not a task to be undertaken lightly, however: failing to pay attention to the points discussed in this chapter can only lead to questionable, if not misleading results and if those results are being used as the basis for service development and improvement, then the service will suffer.

Bibliography

Heather, P., and Stone, S., *Questionnaires*, Sheffield, University of Sheffield Centre for Research on User Studies, [n.d.] (CRUS Guide no. 5).

Hughes, J. A., *Sociological analysis: methods of discovery*, London, Nelson, 1976 (see particularly chapter 6).

Line, M. B., *Library surveys: an introduction to the use, planning, procedure and presentation of surveys*, London, Bingley, 2nd edn, revised by Sue Stone, 1982, (see particularly chapter 3).

Oppenheim, A. N., *Questionnaire design and attitude measurement*, London, Heinemann, 1968.

6 Data analysis and interpretation (quantitative)

Robert Peacock

1. The nature of quantitative data

Quantitative data analysis is concerned with making sense of information in the form of numbers representing counts, ordering or measurements. For example, in a study of the use of a library or information service, you might have information about the following characteristics of the users: sex; age; social class; income; usual time of day for visiting the library/service; length of time spent on a single visit/consultation or sequence of visits; attitude to some aspect of the service, e.g., very pleased, somewhat pleased, indifferent, somewhat displeased, very displeased.

There are many more and different kinds of characteristics of users, and of the information service itself, which might give rise to quantitative data for analysis. The important point is that, if information is quantitative, it can be described, summarized, aggregated, compared and manipulated – in short, analysed and interpreted – in arithmetical ways. This means that it will be possible to use one or more of the four arithmetical operations of addition, subtraction, multiplication and division (or 'ambition, distraction, uglification and derision' in Lewis Carroll's terms) and to use one or more specialized statistical techniques to achieve your aim of identifying and understanding any patterns there might be in your data.

Information and measurement about any characteristic of the natural or social world is variable. Not all users have the same sex, age, interests or attitudes; books come in different sizes and bindings at different prices and published at various times; some sources and authors have more citations over a given period than others. For this reason, characteristics such as those listed are referred to as *variables* and the object of quantitative analysis and interpretation is to reveal any features of commonality between various elements of data within a batch and between batches of data. It should go without saying, should it not, that unless you have a batch of variable data elements, quantitative analysis is a redundant activity. If you have only a single book to consider or a library containing thousands of volumes of the same book, only a single user or a population of cloned users, then everything you might want to know about your library stock or about users might be revealed in a single observation. Fortunately, real-world data is more complex, challenging and interesting than that.

Not all authors start from the fundamental position that counts, orderings and measurements represent quantitative data. One of the examples given above, viz. sex of user, is often referred to as a qualitative variable; after all sex is not measured, is it? Well, maybe not, outside the genetics laboratory or psychology experiment, but it is certainly possible to produce meaningful summaries of numbers of individuals in each of the two categories in the form of counts or proportions and to relate such summary measures to other variables of interest, such as library use. Variables like sex which cannot meaningfully be subtracted, multiplied and divided but merely counted in various named categories, are, naturally, called categorical or nominal variables. We shall see later in the section on relationships and trends, that it is even possible, usual and very useful to perform quite sophisticated tests of comparisons and relationships between categories of nominal variables.

For some variables it makes sense to rank categories of measurement in order. It is common in social research to consider that the order of social class is significant and that the progression, based upon occupation classification, is: professional – intermediate non-manual – skilled manual – unskilled or the same categories in reverse order. When considering user attitudes to a service, 'very pleased' clearly takes precedence over 'indifferent' and 'somewhat displeased'. It makes sense to count numbers of observations in ordered categories and to preserve rank order in the analysis, but it does not make sense to quantify the difference between categories nor to divide one by another and multiply two together.

Measurements such as time taken for a search, age of user, size of book and numbers of citations can be analysed using higher order arithmetical operations than counting and ranking. Because it usually makes sense to interpret differences between observations of such variables, they are called interval data, and if it also makes sense to multiply and divide values they are called ratio data. Many books refer to three distinct 'levels of measurement': nominal, ordinal and interval/ratio, (Marsh 1988, pp. 8–8 and Open University 1983, Unit C1 4.3 p. 22).

This distinction between levels of measurement is not a difficult concept to grasp, but it is fundamental to all quantitative analysis and interpretation. There are specific statistical methods for the analysis of data measured at different levels and it is important to remember that, generally, it is just not possible to use techniques devised for the analysis of interval data in the analysis of ordinal or nominal data, nor for ordinal or ranking methods to be used on pure categories of nominal data. It is, however, perfectly possible and quite common to reduce interval data to an ordered ranking of observations and even to categories. For example, time of arrival in a library might be recorded precisely in terms of hours and minutes, but analysed in terms of (possibly ordered) categories such as morning, afternoon, evening or just early, late. The data collected over an extended period might also be further reduced to counts for days of the week and months of the year.

Data for quantitative analysis always appears as a batch of observations on a variable and as sets of batches of observations on a number of variables. Figure 6.1 illustrates a dataset consisting of at least ten batches, each containing one hundred observations of a variable.

Exercise
Can you identify, in each case, at least one variable in the dataset of figure 6.1 which is purely nominal, ordinal and interval? Are there any variables in the dataset which are qualitative rather than quantitative variables?

Answer
Genre and Imprint are, clearly, mere nominal categories; Month (of publication, presumably) is nominal but also ordinal; Price, numbers of volumes sold Gross, Home and Export and the value of the total Product are all interval scale variables. Title and Author are of course nominal but essentially qualitative variables and it is difficult to see how any meaningful quantitative analysis could be done on the former, though, since there are authors with multiple titles in the list, it would be possible to treat this information quantitatively. Notice that there is information on two other nominal variables embedded in the dataset; the nationality of the author and, almost, the sex of the author. Note that information on author's sex would have to be derived from author's first name and this is neither complete nor unambiguous, e.g., two cases of Anon.; one is E. V. Thompson, another

No.	Title	Genre	Author	Imprint	Price	Month	Home	Export	Gross	Product
1	Rage	Thriller	Wilbur Smith (Br)	Pan	3.99	May	480,173	494,623	974,796	£3,889,436
2	The Parson's Daughter	Saga	Catherine Cookson (Br)	Corgi	3.95	March	621,511	192,638	814,149	£3,215,888
3	Windmill of the Gods	Thriller	Sidney Sheldon (US)	Fontana	3.50	Feb	339,691	311,829	651,520	£2,280,320
4	Savages	Adventure	Shirley Conran (Br)	Pan	3.99	July	418,850	209,600	628,450	£2,507,515
5	Garden of Shadows	Saga	Virginia Andrews (US)	Fontana	3.50	May	380,083	240,827	620,910	£2,173,185
6	Firefly Summer	Novel	Maeve Binchy (Ire)	Coronet	4.50	Oct	391,205	178,472	569,677	£2,563,546
7	Hot Money	Thriller	Dick Francis (Br)	Pan	3.50	Dec	355,110	211,934	567,044	£1,984,654
8	Dirk Gently's . . . Agency	Humour	Douglas Adams (Br)	Pan	2.99	June	352,674	202,903	555,577	£1,661,175
9	Destiny	Saga	Sally Beauman (Br)	Corgi	3.95	April	387,577	154,035	541,612	£2,139,367
10	Sepulchre	Horror	James Herbert (Br)	NEL	3.50	June	383,665	148,904	532,569	£1,863,991
11	Misery	Horror	Stephen King (US)	NEL	3.50	Nov	331,488	171,364	502,852	£1,759,982
12	Bill Bailey's Lot	Saga	Catherine Cookson (Br)	Corgi	2.99	Oct	413,951	71,676	485,627	£1,452,024
13	Winter	Novel	Len Deighton (Br)	Grafton	3.99	Nov	263,176	220,275	483,451	£1,928,969
14	Pearls	Novel	Celia Brayfield (Br)	Penguin	3.95	Nov	288,891	151,070	439,961	£1,737,845
15	Hip & Thigh Diet	Health	Rosemary Conley (Br)	Arrow	2.50	Jan	360,878	70,241	431,119	£1,077,797
16	Ladies of Missolonghi	Novel	Colleen McCullogh (Aus)	Arrow	2.50	March	179,091	250,783	429,874	£1,074,685
17	Fine Things	Romance	Danielle Steel (US)	Sphere	3.50	July	338,613	43,439	382,052	£1,337,182
18	Neighbours: Behind . . .	TV Tie-in	James Oram (Aus)	Angus & R	3.95	Aug	319,980	47,500	367,480	£1,451,546
19	Red Storm Rising	Fiction	Tom Clancy (US)	Fontana	3.95	Jan	201,354	158,015	359,369	£1,419,507
20	The Eyes of the Dragon	Horror	Stephen King (US)	Futura	3.50	Jan	225,256	112,369	337,625	£1,181,687
21	The Weeping & Laughter	Novel	Noel Barber (Br)	Coronet	3.99	Dec	191,527	125,833	317,360	£1,266,266
22	Winter Hawk	Thriller	Craig Thomas (US)	Fontana	3.95	April	191,207	123,389	314,596	£1,242,654
23	Kaleidoscope	Romance	Danielle Steel (US)	Sphere	3.99	Dec	233,914	74,442	308,356	£1,230,340
24	Weaveworld	Novel	Clive Barker (Br)	Fontana	3.95	Aug	218,115	86,203	304,318	£1,202,056
25	Superhoroscopes '89	Astrology	Anon (Br)	Arrow	2.99	June	181,100	120,909	302,009	£903,006
26	Presumed Innocent	Novel	Scott Turow (US)	Penguin	3.99	Oct	199,514	99,670	299,184	£1,193,744
27	Patriot Games	Novel	Tom Clancy (US)	Fontana	3.95	Nov	165,517	132,994	298,511	£1,179,118
28	Glittering Images	Novel	Susan Howatch (Br)	Fontana	3.95	June	179,331	112,720	292,051	£1,153,601
29	At Close Quarters	Thriller	Gerald Seymour (Br)	Fontana	3.50	Oct	179,771	103,698	283,469	£992,141
30	Horoscopes 1989	Astrology	Anon (Br)	Grafton	1.99	Aug	71,856	198,288	270,144	£537,586
31	Wolf Winter	Thriller	Clare Francis (Br)	Pan	3.99	Nov	150,865	106,060	256,925	£1,025,130
32	The Janus Man	Thriller	Colin Forbes (Br)	Pan	2.95	Jan	149,514	97,665	247,179	£729,178
33	Sarum	Novel	Edward Rutherford (Br)	Arrow	3.50	June	174,692	68,837	243,529	£852,351
34	Shan	Thriller	Eric Van Lustbader (US)	Grafton	3.95	May	117,707	123,649	241,356	£953,356
35	Janet	Humour	Smith & Jones (Br)	Fontana	4.50	Oct	223,643	3,431	227,074	£1,021,833
36	The Fatal Shore	History	Robert Hughes (Aus)	Pan	4.99	April	81,227	140,742	221,969	£1,107,625
37	Wildacre	Novel	Philippa Gregory (Br)	Penguin	3.95	March	151,932	56,560	208,492	£823,543
38	The Golden Girls	Saga	Elvi Rhodes (Br)	Corgi	3.95	Feb	186,251	18,922	205,173	£810,433
39	Yes Mama	Novel	Helen Forrester (Br)	Fontana	3.50	Nov	175,504	28,569	204,073	£714,255
40	Jig	Thriller	Campbell Armstrong (Br)	Coronet	3.95	Aug	139,691	61,389	201,080	£794,266
41	Washington Wives	Novel	Maureen Dean (US)	Grafton	3.50	July	117,719	83,165	200,884	£703,094
42	Unforgettable Fire: U2	Music	Eamon Dunphy (Ire)	Penguin	3.99	Nov	125,392	74,649	200,041	£798,163
43	The Legacy	Saga	Linda de Plante (Br)	Pan	3.99	Oct	92,244	97,252	189,496	£756,089
44	Communion	Misc	Whitley Strieber (US)	Arrow	3.50	Feb	80,457	105,925	186,382	£652,337
45	Talking to Strange Men	Crime	Ruth Rendell (Br)	Arrow	2.99	Sep	107,843	70,898	178,741	£534,435
46	The Dandelion Seed	Novel	Lena Kennedy (Br)	Futura	3.50	Aug	171,718	6,113	177,831	£622,408
47	Heaven & Hell	Novel	John Jakes (US)	Fontana	4.95	Dec	80,544	97,246	177,790	£880,060
48	Voyage	Novel	Elizabeth Walker (US)	Headline	3.50	July	116,332	60,752	177,084	£619,794
49	The Mother's Daughter	Novel	Marilyn French (US)	Pan	4.99	Nov	96,299	74,730	171,029	£853,434
50	Sisters	Novel	Pat Booth (Br)	Arrow	3.50	April	64,350	101,597	165,947	£580,814
51	Hermit of Eyton Forest	Crime	Ellis Peters (Br)	Futura	2.99	July	149,271	16,027	165,298	£494,241
52	Daughter of the Empire	Fantasy	Feist & Wurts (US)	Grafton	3.99	Oct	110,344	54,909	165,253	£659,359
53	The Radiant Way	Novel	Margaret Drabble (Br)	Penguin	3.95	Oct	123,759	38,483	162,242	£640,855
54	Silk Vendetta	Romance	Victoria Holt (Br)	Fontana	3.95	Sep	91,618	68,965	160,583	£634,302
55	Moon Tiger	Novel	Penelope Lively (Br)	Penguin	3.99	Oct	126,860	28,617	155,477	£620,353
56	The Dark Tower	Fantasy	Stephen King (US)	Sphere	6.99	Sep	102,299	52,178	154,477	£1,079,794
57	Dingbats	Misc	Paul Sellers (Br)	Corgi	1.99	Oct	152,667	223	152,890	£304,251
58	Outbreak	Horror	Robin Cook (US)	Pan	2.99	April	68,733	83,484	152,217	£455,128
59	Mort	Fantasy	Terry Pratchett (Br)	Corgi	2.99	Nov	127,400	24,533	151,933	£454,279
60	Wicked Willie	Humour	Jolliffe & Mayle (Br)	Pan	3.99	Oct	136,399	15,416	151,815	£605,741
61	Seventh Sanctuary	Thriller	Daniel Easterman (Br)	Grafton	3.95	July	59,353	91,138	150,491	£594,439
62	Watchers	Thriller	Dean R. Koontz (US)	Headline	3.50	May	87,970	61,323	149,293	£522,525
63	Under Eye of Clock	Autobiog	Christopher Nolan (Ire)	Pan	2.99	Oct	95,816	50,755	146,571	£438,247
64	Secret for Nightingale	Romance	Victoria Holt (Br)	Fontana	3.50	March	78,699	66,905	145,604	£509,614
65	First Lady	Novel	Erin Pizzey (Br)	Fontana	3.95	July	72,218	71,798	144,016	£568,863
66	Dreams Are Not Enough	Novel	Jacqueline Briskin (US)	Corgi	3.95	May	74,055	69,431	143,486	£566,769
67	Peace on Earth	Thriller	Gordon Stevens (Br)	Coronet	3.50	March	51,220	89,158	140,378	£491,323
68	The Looney	Novel	Spike Milligan (Br)	Penguin	2.99	Oct	125,812	12,667	138,479	£414,052
69	The Stricken Land	Saga	E. V. Thompson (Br)	Pan	2.99	Feb	97,132	35,901	133,033	£397,768
70	The Past is Myself	Autobiog	Christabel Bielenberg (Br)	Corgi	3.95	Nov	130,443	1,936	132,379	£522,897
71	Are You Lonesome . . .	Misc	Barbin & Matera (US)	Arrow	3.50	Oct	45,662	85,653	131,315	£459,602
72	Something to Fall . . .	Humour	Maureen Lipman (Br)	Futura	3.50	Oct	127,186	530	127,716	£447,006
73	Cold New Dawn	Novel	Ian St James (Br)	Fontana	3.95	July	66,921	60,058	126,979	£501,567
74	Bros Fact File	Pop	Bros (Br)	Fantail	3.99	Oct	120,250	6,723	126,973	£506,622
75	First Born	Novel	Doris Mortman (US)	Coronet	3.99	Nov	83,952	41,742	125,694	£501,519
76	The Rotation Diet	Health	Martin Katahn (US)	Corgi	3.50	Jan	94,188	31,159	125,347	£438,714
77	Shadows on the Snow	Fiction	Madge Swindells (SA)	Futura	3.50	March	99,856	25,175	125,031	£437,608
78	Fatherhood	Autobiog	Bill Cosby (US)	Bantam	2.50	March	72,335	50,706	123,041	£307,602
79	Honour This Day	Adventure	Alexander Kent (Br)	Pan	3.50	July	85,673	35,359	121,032	£423,612
80	Fiddler's Ferry	Saga	Iris Gower (Br)	Corgi	3.50	June	110,992	9,424	120,416	£421,456
81	Prince of Tides	Novel	Pat Conroy (Br)	Bantam	3.95	April	70,308	49,542	119,850	£473,407
82	Daughter of Northern . . .	Novel	Pamela Haines (Br)	Fontana	3.95	Aug	84,277	35,026	119,303	£471,246
83	Day of Creation	Novel	J. G. Ballard (Br)	Grafton	2.99	Sep	77,153	41,747	118,900	£355,511
84	Not That Sort of Girl	Novel	Mary Wesley (Br)	Black S	3.95	July	110,558	8,150	118,708	£468,896
85	Dangerous in Love	Novel	Leslie Thomas (Br)	Penguin	2.99	Nov	100,332	15,874	116,206	£347,456
86	Going Solo	Autobiog	Roald Dahl (Br)	Penguin	3.99	Nov	99,311	16,097	115,408	£460,477
87	Over the Edge	Thriller	Jonathan Kellerman (US)	Futura	3.50	May	71,207	43,800	115,007	£402,524
88	Erin's Child	Romance	Sheelagh Kelly (Br)	Arrow	3.99	May	91,282	23,188	114,470	£456,735
89	Floyd in Britain . . .	Cookery	Keith Floyd (Br)	BBC Books	7.95	Sep	110,185	3,000	113,185	£899,820
90	League of Night & Fog	Thriller	David Morrell (US)	NEL	3.99	Oct	59,994	52,971	112,965	£450,730
91	Pussy Pie Hits Town	Humour	Jolliffe & Graham (Br)	Pan	3.99	Nov	99,287	12,861	112,148	£447,470
92	A Fatal Inversion	Crime	Barbara Vine (Br)	Penguin	3.50	Dec	75,603	36,372	111,975	£391,912
93	The Hearts . . . of Men	Novel	Fay Weldon (Br)	Fontana	3.95	Sep	64,969	46,863	111,832	£441,736
94	Riches	Novel	Una-Mary Parker (Br)	Headline	3.50	June	56,423	55,336	111,759	£391,156
95	All My Wordly Goods	Romance	Anne Weale (Br)	Arrow	3.99	Sep	58,115	52,730	110,845	£442,271
96	Stalker	Autobiog	John Stalker (Br)	Penguin	3.50	Oct	98,748	11,149	109,897	£384,639
97	Summer Visitors	Saga	Susan Sallis (Br)	Corgi	2.95	May	98,512	10,652	109,164	£322,033
98	It's All in the . . .	Autobiog	Shirley Maclaine (US)	Bantam	3.99	Aug	47,224	61,576	108,800	£434,112
99	East Wind	Saga	Julie Ellis (Br)	Grafton	3.50	Oct	73,147	33,619	106,766	£373,681
100	Flight of the Old Dog	Thriller	Dale Brown (US)	Grafton	3.50	Aug	63,578	41,907	105,485	£369,197

Source: *Guardian*, Friday 13 Jan 1989 p. 23

Fig. 6.1 Millionaire's row: 1988's top-selling softback writers in Britain

J. G. Ballard; one Bros; several cases such as Smith & Jones, Feist & Wurts; and what sex do first names like Elvi and Dale imply?

It is important with any data to note exactly what it purports to represent and what it does not. In this case it is for *softback* sales in *Britain* in *1988* (presumably from 1 January to 31 December inclusive). If you are interested in sales of hardback books or any other kind of media or information service, or of softback sales in other years or countries, this dataset would be quite useless. Note that the batches of data are presented in rank order in terms of the total numbers of volumes of each title sold Gross and not in terms of Product value, Author, Imprint, or Genre. If you are interested in that kind of information you will have to do some quantitative analysis of your own.

2. The role of the computer in quantitative data analysis

Electronic computers used for quantitative data analysis have been available since the Second World War, but the advent of the desktop personal computer, during the late 1970s, revolutionized the capability and facility for research users to store, manipulate, retrieve, present and analyse their own or others' data. This has been partly due to the increasing operation speed and data storage capacity of microcomputers; partly due to dramatically falling prices of about 30% per year during the 1980s leading to a halving of systems' prices in real terms at approximately two-yearly intervals; partly due to the development of microcomputer operating systems with 'friendly' user interfaces (the automatic presentation on screen of text and graphic information enabling the user to interact with the computer hardware and, more importantly, the data analysis program or other software it is running) which led to greater computer awareness in a wide population of educational, business, research and home users and an extension of individuals' skills; partly, and not least, to the development of software packages which are easy to use, flexible, sophisticated in their facilities and also subject to falling prices.

These trends have, without doubt, revolutionized data analysis. During the 1960s, researchers not employed in major research institutions used traditional methods of data analysis involving the tallying and summing of data by hand, eye and brain, the calculation of proportions and multiplications using relatively imprecise slide rules and tables of logarithms or large, slow and expensive mechanical tabulators. In the 1970s, statistical analysis using pencil and paper was greatly facilitated, speeded up and made more accurate by the electronic calculator, first desktop then pocket size. Researchers of the 1990s will have all the advanced facilities of modern desktop computing, developed during the previous decade, plus the capability of receiving and transmitting data quickly and cheaply electronically by FAX or over digital networks, to communicate with remote databases and to acquire personal databases stored on read/write floppy disks or read only CD-ROM compact disks and random access video disks.

Researchers will always do quick mental calculations with the aid of a pencil and on the back of an envelope, in the margin of a book or on computer printout, to get a quick estimate, make a comparison, test an idea, sketch a trend or possible relationship; and it is right that they should do so (Marsh 1988 p. 198). It has become so easy and quick to summarize fairly large datasets, to perform statistical calculations and make tests and to present the data and the results of comparisons in tables, charts and graphs using powerful graphics software and laser printers for the highest quality of presentation. Most of the examples given in later sections of this chapter were produced within seconds, using not very powerful mid-1980s pc technology but with a very powerful and flexible interactive data analysis package, Minitab; some examples took a few minutes to produce, no more. What is much more difficult than manipulating the numbers and presenting the output, what is the heart of analysis, is seeking and asking the right questions about the data and interpreting the results, i.e., forming correct or valid judgements about the answers obtained in relation to the original questions. This is not a skill which can be taught, although the principles can; it must be learned by doing, and this is why all four key references given at the end of this chapter emphasize repetitive practice on many different batches of data and datasets. The more important skill for a researcher is not the ability to do statistics but the ability to understand the data itself and to ask relevant questions about the data which analysis might help to answer.

There are many academically and commercially successful software packages for the analysis and presentation of quantitative data. Four of these, which you are very likely to have seen reference to, are: SPSS (Statistical Package for the Social Sciences), Minitab, Lotus 1-2-3 and DBase IV.

The first two were originally available on large, institutional mainframe computer installations and analysis was performed in batch process, whereby at a particular stage in the analysis the researcher would select all the data of interest and decide on all the manipulations and form of output required before submitting it to the computer for remote processing. During the 1980s, interactive versions of these programs enabled the researcher to sit at a terminal and 'play' with the data by trying 'look see' or 'what if?' calculations, thus facilitating understanding and interesting discovery of patterns in the data by serendipity. Later on, the speed and storage capacity of personal computers advanced so that these programs could be used under desktop control by the researcher. The other two pieces of software are examples of two very important generic forms of data handling which were developed specifically for use on personal computers, the spreadsheet (Lotus) and database (DBIV). Although the ways in which these different kinds of programs store, manipulate and output data are conceptually different, they all enable the researcher to analyse data and present it in similar ways. What you use will be determined by what is available and what you feel comfortable with.

3. Data reduction and presentation

The essence of data analysis is the development of an understanding of the information it contains. Where the data is quantitative that means making sense of all the various numbers and the patterns they form. Ideally, the aim should be to understand everything about the various batches available and their relationships, if any, one to another or others. But this aim will be limited by time, expense, imagination and judgement about just how much it is important to understand about the data in order to satisfactorlly answer the key research questions. Of course, one of the challenging and exciting aspects of data analysis is that it is rarely possible to know, once and for all, exactly what is relevant, what are proper questions and what is valid interpretation (Marsh 1988 p. 154).

The first stage in quantitative analysis is to reduce possibly large batches and datasets, which can be very confusing in the mass of numbers, to tabular and graphical forms and numerical summaries which enable the researcher either to identify possible questions to ask about observed patterns, or to begin to formulate strategies for working towards answers to previously identified questions. In figure 6.1 the four columns concerned with sales and value of sales contain 400 distinct quantities represented by some 2,400 separate digits. This is all very confusing and difficult to make sense of. If there are any interesting patterns in the figures it should be possible to tease them out by an analysis of no more than about 800 of the digits.

Ehrenberg (1975 pp. 3–5) argues that when reading data from a table it is only possible to take in and mentally compare figures with a maximum of two digits. He provides many examples of effective tabular presentation based on this principle. It is common to refer to the important digits for presentation and comparison as significant figures; Marsh (1988 p. 8) introduces the idea of varying digits and argues that it is rarely necessary to produce tables with more than two. In figure 6.1 the column for Gross sales contains figures with six varying digits; these should be reduced to two, e.g., from the top: 970,000; 810,000; 650,000 etc. The column for Product contains figures with six or seven varying digits and here it would be necessary to retain two or three in each case. The adjusted figures can be obtained by cutting or rounding the originals, e.g., the fourth figure in the Gross sales column could be cut to 620,000 or rounded to 630,000. In practice it is not likely to matter very much which method is used provided it is done correctly, but cutting is intuitively easy to understand, quick to do and less prone to error, compared to rounding.

It is not possible to analyse here all of the data in figure 6.1 in depth. For the many different ways in which these numerous observations on several variables might be summarized, tabulated and displayed graphically, you should refer to Marsh and Ehrenberg. If you have access to a personal computer and suitable software such as Minitab, you can derive many summaries and displays very quickly either on screen, or using a printer in hard copy.

There are some examples of the results of applying some Minitab data summary commands to figure 6.1 given in figure 6.2.

Figure 6.2 presents ten summary measures for four of the interval scale variables, which were produced by asking Minitab to DESCRIBE them. The letter N refers to the total number of observations in each variable batch.

MEAN is the arithmetic mean, commonly known as the average, of each batch, which is obtained by adding up all the data values and dividing by N − notice that the means do not have any decimal fraction part, which you might expect, so Minitab must have cut or rounded the figure, probably the latter.

```
MTB > describe 'home' 'export' 'gross' 'product'

             N      MEAN    MEDIAN    TRMEAN     STDEV   SEMEAN
Home       100    160283    117713    149377    112888    11289
Export     100     82316     61482     74491     76079     7608
Gross      100    242599    165622    222555    170633    17063
Product    100    896385    628355    817166    652616    65262

            MIN       MAX        Q1        Q3
Home      45662    621511     81908    189968
Export      223    494623     33971    106026
Gross    105485    974796    125434    301303
Product  304251   3889436    454491   1142107
```

RAP(OU)

Fig. 6.2 Minitab data summary commands

It is also clear that the program must be working with all the given digits and not just two significant or varying ones. It is important to do that in calculations and to round only the final result. Of course it is no problem for a computer to work with massive numbers of digits – no hed, so no headache.

The MEDIAN is an extremely important summary statistic, especially in EDA or exploratory data analysis which is the subject of the next section below; it is that value of the variable which divides the batch in two so that, in this case, there must be 50 observations with values greater than the median and 50 with values less. You can see that in each case, the value of the median is quite a bit less than the mean. That is because the median value is much less sensitive than the mean is to the presence of a few very large values in the batch. For this reason the median is said to be a more *resistant* measure of the average level of data values in a batch to the overall shape of the distribution of values, compared to the mean.

TRMEAN represents a trimmed mean, i.e., a mean for 90% of the values with the top and bottom 5% excluded. These values are closer to the median but still quite a long way away. STDEV (standard deviation) and SEMEAN (standard error of the mean) are measures which are important in connection with comparisons between samples and making tests of statistical significance which will be considered in sections 6 and 7.

MIN and MAX are, naturally, the greatest and least values in each batch, called E_L the lower extreme and E_U the upper extreme in some texts (Open University 1983). Q_1 and Q_3 are the lower and upper quartiles respectively, which mark off the lowest 25% and the highest 25% of data values. The median corresponds to Q_2, the second quartile in the distribution of values in the batch.

Taken together, the median with the quartiles, or the mean with the standard deviation provide a summary of the distribution of values in the batch. It is also useful to picture the distribution graphically and a common way of doing this is to prepare a bar chart or histogram. These two representations are very similar, though not the same, as you will see by reference to Marsh or Ehrenberg.

Figure 6.3 presents Minitab versions of the histograms for home and export sales of softbacks in 1988. These displays show that most home sales (34%) were in the range 75,000–125,000 whilst most export sales were in the range 25,000–75,000, about 50,000 less on average which agrees with a comparison of medians in figure 6.2, but not of means which are affected quite

```
MTB > hist 'home 'export'
Histogram of home    N = 100

Midpoint    Count
   50000      19    *******************
  100000      34    **********************************
  150000      16    ****************
  200000      12    ************
  250000       3    ***
  300000       2    **
  350000       6    ******
  400000       6    ******
  450000       0
  500000       1    *
  550000       0
  600000       1    *

Histogram of export   N = 100
Midpoint    Count
       0      20    ********************
   50000      42    ******************************************
  100000      19    *****************
  150000       8    ********
  200000       7    *******
  250000       2    **
  300000       1    *
  350000       0
  400000       0
  450000       0
  500000       1    *
```

RAP(OU)

Fig. 6.3   Minitab histogram home and export sales

a lot by the 14% of home sales greater than 325,000 volumes, compared to only 1% of export sales greater than that amount.

A rather more dramatic and revealing illustration of the difference between the batches of home and export sales in terms of level, spread and shape of the overall distribution is shown by Minitab dotplots drawn to the same scale and presented as figure 6.4:

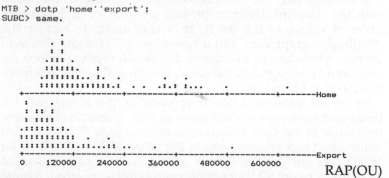

RAP(OU)

Fig. 6.4   Minitab dotplot home and export sales

Notice that every dot on the plot represents one value of the home sales or export sales of a particular title. The plot shows dramatically what is already known about the medians and quartiles of the two distributions, cf. figure 6.2, that rather less than 25% of export sales are of more than 120,000 volumes per title, whereas more than 50% of home sales are of more than 120,000 volumes per title.

4. Exploratory data analysis

Exploratory data analysis (EDA) refers to the crucial, initial stages of any research study with data to be analysed. More precisely, EDA embodies a set of techniques for displaying batches of data in ways which facilitate the perception of any interesting patterns in the batch and of possible relationships between variables in two or more batches of data, whilst always retaining as much as possible of the data contained in the raw data values. These techniques were pioneered by the eminent American statistician, John Tukey, and provide the basis for the approach to data analysis taken by Marsh (1988) and Open University (1983). The analysis program Minitab contains several commands which enable EDA to be applied to a set of data.

First, take a look at the EDA version of histograms for the data on home and export sales for the set of 100 softback titles. These are called stem-and-leaf plots, or just *stemplots*, and can be produced by Minitab in response to the command STEM-AND-LEAF, or just STEM, followed by the variable name or names of interest. The result is shown in figure 6.5.

Exercise

Look at the stemplots of figure 6.5 and consider how they compare with the histograms of figure 6.3.

Answer

The shapes of the two different displays are very similar, though not exactly the same. Both displays plot 100 data points; the histogram plots them as anonymous asterisks, the stemplot as digits.

On the left of the histogram there is a scale showing the midpoint value of intervals within which the data values have been plotted; in the centre there is a column showing a count of the number of data values falling in each interval and from the histogram for home sales it is possible to deduce that the median value seems to fall close to the upper limit of the 75,000–125,000 range of sales.

```
MTB > stem 'home' 'export'

Stem-and-leaf of home        N  = 100
Leaf Unit = 10000


     2    0  44
    41    0  5555566666777777777888888889999999999999
  (22)    1  0001111111222222233344
    37    1  555677777788999
    22    2  01223
    17    2  68
    15    3  1333
    11    3  5568889
     4    4  11
     2    4  8
     1    5
     1    5
     1    6  2

Stem-and-leaf of export      N  = 100
Leaf Unit = 10000


    38    0  0000000001111111112222233333344444444
  (34)    0  5555555566666666677777778888899999
    28    1  0000112222344
    15    1  5557799
     8    2  00124
     3    2  5
     2    3  1
     1    3
     1    4
     1    4  9
```

RAP(OU)

Fig. 6.5 Minitab stemplot home and export sales

The essence of the stemplot is that it displays all the varying digits for each of the 100 data values in the batch, after cutting. In this case the lowest four varying digits of the numbers of home sales have been cut leaving just one or two varying digits. The first varying digit of each data value appears on the stem of the plot and the second varying digit appears as a leaf. The stem is represented by the central column of the plot and the leaves by the rows of figures extending to the right at each level. A caption to the display explains that in this case a leaf unit has the value 10,000, so the two titles with the lowest numbers of home sales appear to have sold 04 × 10,000 volumes each, i.e., 40,000 volumes, whereas the titles with the greatest number of home sales are shown as having sold 62 × 10,000, i.e., 620,000 volumes. Reference to figure 6.1 reveals that the actual uncut values for the home sales of these titles were 45,662, 47,224 and 621,511 respectively.

Minitab presents all the leaf values in order and in addition a column on the left of the display which shows the 'depth' of each leaf counting up from the bottom of the distribution and down from the top. The stem level which contains the value of the median has the number of observations at that level shown enclosed in parentheses.

These features make it very easy to pick out estimates of the medians and quartiles from stemplots. With 100 data values an estimate of the median lies between the 50th and 51st observations in rank order; the lower quartile, Q_1, between 25th and 26th; the upper quartile, Q_2, between 75th and 76th. From the plot for home sales it is possible to quickly find estimates of 80,000, 110,000 and 180,000 for Q_1, Median and Q_2, and for export sales the estimates 30,000, 60,000 and 100,000 respectively. These are, of course, cut values which are reasonably close to their corresponding computed values shown in figure 6.1, which were: 81,908 117, 713 189,968 and 33,971 61,482 106,026.

EDA also includes a technique for displaying the main features of a distribution of data values graphically, including identification of median and quartiles and extreme values, which provides a useful summary of the information contained in the dotplots of figure 6.4. The EDA display is called a *boxplot*, or box-and-whisker because of its appearance. Figure 6.6 was produced using the Minitab command BOXPLOT for home sales and export sales:

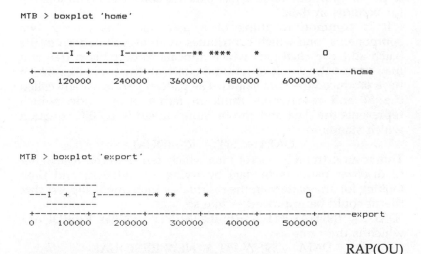

```
MTB > boxplot 'home'

        -----------
    ---I   +      I-------------** ****    *            0
        -----------
  +---------+---------+---------+---------+---------+------home
  0    120000    240000    360000    480000    600000



MTB > boxplot 'export'

        ----------
    ---I   +   I----------* **      *              0
        ----------
  +---------+---------+---------+---------+---------+------export
  0    100000    200000    300000    400000    500000
```

RAP(OU)

Fig. 6.6 Minitab boxplot home and export sales

A boxplot presents a lot of useful information about the distribution of data values. On the Minitab output it should be easy to identify the 'box' and the 'whiskers' extending from the end of each box and represented by a dashed line. Within the box a plus sign (+) marks the position of the median and the ends of the box represent the lower and upper quartiles. This means that 50% of the variable batch values lie with the interval defined by the box. Certain extreme values are indicated by * and 0 symbols. For further detail and discussion about the interpretation of whiskers and extreme values, you should refer to Marsh (1988, pp. 110–13) and to Open University (1983, Units A0,A1,A2).

EDA provides an extremely valuable set of techniques and although a computer is useful it is not necessary in order to prepare stemplots and boxplots fairly quickly for batches of data containing less than 50 values. You should practise doing this with pencil and paper, using the examples and datasets provided in the references and especially with your own data.

5. Relationships and trends

Research is often concerned with discovering and quantifying relationships between variables, with establishing to what extent the values of one variable might be predicted from given values of another and with how reliable a measure of the relationship might be. Looking for and identifying relationships between variables, and trends in one or more variables over time, is an important part of data analysis which is concerned with looking for patterns in data.

It is common to think of a data value as having two components, one which contributes to an overall pattern in the batch and a *residual* part which appears to be pattern free and may be just the result of random effects in the processes which have produced the data values. The pattern part is usually called the *fit* and researchers think in terms of a model which represents the data and can be summarized in a DFR equation which stands for:

DATA = FIT + RESIDUAL

This is an extremely useful idea which can help the researcher to discover patterns in data by trying an initial fit and then looking for any pattern in the residuals which might suggest that the fit could be improved – like so:

DATA = INITIAL FIT + RESIDUAL FIT + NEW RESIDUAL

which is the same as:

DATA = NEW FIT + NEW RESIDUAL

and so on.

For many examples of the use of the method in many different contexts and with different kinds of data, see Marsh (1988) and Open University (1983).

Relationships can be explored between nominal variables, ordinal variables and interval/ratio scale variables. The techniques of presentation and summarizing vary depending upon the type of data being analysed. Figure 6.7 is an example of a scatter diagram, also referred to as a *scattergram* or *scatterplot*, which was produced by the Minitab PLOT command to display the data values for home sales and export sales of 100 titles on the same diagram, in order to reveal whether there is any evidence of a relationship between the two.

A detailed description of how to draw your own scatterplot by hand and how to interpret the result is given in Open University (1983, A3 pp. 6–12). The Minitab program has plotted all 100 pairs of data values, but because at the scale of presentation so many of them lie very close together a number representing approximate values has been printed instead of the separate observations. The particular pattern observed in figure 6.7 does suggest that there is a relationship between export sales and home sales.

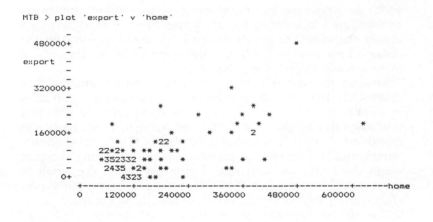

RAP(OU)

Fig. 6.7 Minitab scatterplot home and export sales

Notice that high values of export sales tend to be associated with high values of home sales and vice versa; this is called a positive relationship. The relationship is not perfect, however. If it were, you would expect all of the points in the plot to lie on a straight line. There is a considerable amount of residual scatter around any line which might be chosen to fit the apparent relationship.

Minitab has also computed a statistical summary measure of the relationship represented by the scatterplot. This is the *correlation coefficient* which has a value of +0.616. If all the points in the plot fell on an upwardly sloping straight line the correlation would have the maximum possible value of +1.0; if they all fell on a downward sloping straight line the correlation would be −1.0; a correlation of zero, 0.0, indicates that there is no evidence from the scatter that any relationship between the two variables could be summarized by a straight line, though there could be other forms of relationship (Marsh 1988). In short, if there is in fact *no* relationship between two variables then the correlation coefficient will be zero; however, if the correlation *is* zero, there may or may not be a substantive relationship between the variables and that would require further investigation with the help of the DFR equation.

Many interesting batches of data occur as time series; the individual values relate to fixed, evenly spaced time intervals such as days, weeks, months or years. There are many sophisticated techniques for analysing time-series data which enable the identification of patterns representing trend in the observations, seasonal patterns and other recurring patterns, if there are any (Marsh 1988 chapter 9).

As ever, the first step in the analysis is to present the data graphically. In figure 6.8 the plots of home sales and export sales by month of publication are shown. It is important to note that total sales during the year of all titles published in a particular month are a function of both the number of titles published that month and the number of months remaining during the year when the books were on sale. Figure 6.8 shows the result of using Minitab command TSPLOT to look at home and export sales during 1988 of titles published month by month.

The numbers of titles in the dataset (not shown on plot) by month of publication are:

Jan.− 5   Feb.− 4   Mar.−7   Apr.− 6   May− 8   Jun.−7
Jul.− 10   Aug.−8   Sep.−7   Oct.−19   Nov.−14   Dec.−5

The patterns are rather different between the two time series.

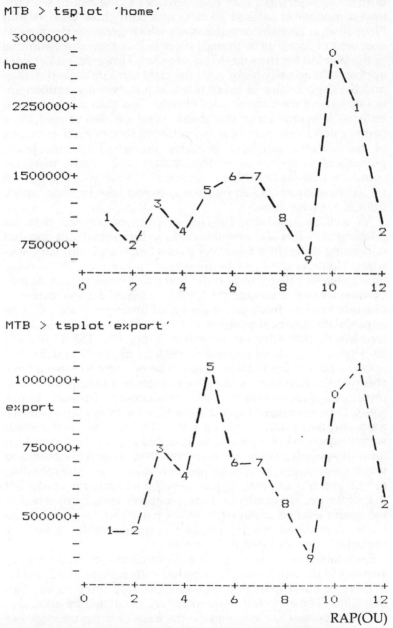

Fig. 6.8 **Home and export sales by month of publication**

Both show September with its seven titles as the month with the lowest number of sales of its titles and both show October and November as months of publication which generate the highest numbers of sales, even though there is less than three months of the year left for the sales to be recorded. However, export sales appear to be actually highest for the eight titles published in May and the export sales of those titles, at just over one million are not far behind their home sales of rather less than one and a half million. It seems clear that book sales are determined by a complicated interaction of many different factors such as month of publication, numbers of titles published, genre, price, publishers' assessment of the market and many more. A complete analysis of softback sales in 1988, even with the limited information contained in figure 6.1, would take far more space than is available here.

As well as analysing batches of pairs of interval data for relationships, it is also possible to do so for ordinal and nominal data using different methods of presentation and summary statistics. Nominal data can be presented in the form of two-way tables of their categories and the pattern of observations distributed between the various categories examined for any evidence of a relationship. Such tables are called *contingency tables* and an appropriate statistical measure of relationship is called *chi-square* (see Marsh 1988 Chapter 7, Section 5, pp. 128–130, Ehrenberg 1975 pp. 335–6, Open University 1983, B3 pp. 9–13 and 20–36).

In the book sales dataset it would be possible to form a table showing the numbers of titles by, say, genre and imprint and to investigate the pattern for any relationship. Instead figures 6.9–6.11 present three small 2 × 2 tables, i.e. tables with just two rows and two columns giving four cells, derived from a small survey of readers of a pamphlet designed to provide information for older people. There are three variables: useful, learned and vimpt (very important), with just two values 1,2 corresponding to YES and NO answers to questions: (a) whether the reader felt that older people would find the pamphlet useful; (b) whether the reader learned anything from the pamphlet; (c) whether the reader considered any information in the pamphlet to be very important for older people to know.

Each table shows the distribution of counts of all 54 sets of answers in the small sample, together with expected frequencies if there is no relationship between the responses to the two questions. The expected frequencies are calculated by allocating the 54 responses to categories on the basis of the proportions of responses to each question which are shown in the ALL categories row at the foot of the table and the ALL categories column on the right hand side. The difference between the actual count in each cell and the expected frequency provides the basis for making a judgement about whether the observed pattern is sufficiently different from the expected frequencies based on an assumption of no relationship in order to conclude that there is some evidence that there is a relationship.

```
ROWS: useful        COLUMNS: learned

              1          2        ALL

   1         18         23         41
          15.94      25.06      41.00

   2          3         10         13
           5.06       7.94      13.00

  ALL        21         33         54
          21.00      33.00      54.00

CHI-SQUARE =      1.801   WITH D.F. =      1
   CELL CONTENTS --
                    COUNT
                    EXP FREQ                    RAP(OU)
```

Fig. 6.9 Chi-square useful/learned

```
ROWS: vimpt         COLUMNS: useful

              1          2        ALL

   1         35          9         44
          33.41      10.59      44.00

   2          6          4         10
           7.59       2.41      10.00

  ALL        41         13         54
          41.00      13.00      54.00

CHI-SQUARE =      1.703   WITH D.F. =      1
   CELL CONTENTS --
                    COUNT
                    EXP FREQ                    RAP(OU)
```

Fig. 6.10 Chi-square vimpt/useful

```
ROWS: vimpt        COLUMNS: learned

              1        2        ALL

   1         21       23        44
          17.11    26.89     44.00

   2          0       10        10
           3.89     6.11     10.00

 ALL         21       33        54
          21.00    33.00     54.00

CHI-SQUARE =        7.810    WITH D.F. =     1
   CELL CONTENTS --
                    COUNT
                    EXP FREQ
```
                                              RAP(OU)

Fig. 6.11 Chi-square vimpt/learned

The statistic chi-square provides a summary of the overall difference in pattern between the observed and expected frequencies. If the calculated value of chi-square for a particular table turns out to be greater than a specified value, then it is possible to conclude that there is evidence of a statistically significant relationship.

For a 2 × 2 table the specified value of chi-square is 3.8 (derived from published tables). Because the value computed for figure 6.9 is 1.8, less than 3.8, it is possible to say that there is no evidence of any relationship between whether the readers learned anything from the pamphlet and whether they felt it would be useful for older people. Similarly for figure 6.10, chi-square = 1.7 which is less than 3.8 so there is no evidence of any relationship between answers about usefulness of the pamphlet and whether it was considered to contain anything very important for older people to know. The third table, however, shown in figure 6.11, has a large chi-square value of 7.8 from which it might be possible to conclude that answers about whether the pamphlet is considered to contain information very important for older people are related to answers about whether the reader learned anything from it. There is an important proviso though; one of the expected frequencies is 3.89 and the chi-square test of relationship is not considered to be very reliable if any of the expected frequencies turn out to be less than 5. For more on all this you should consult the Open University reference. There is more on sampling and statistical significance tests in the next two sections.

6. Surveys, samples and estimation

Most research is concerned with analysing data in batches representing a larger superbatch. A common term for a superbatch is the *target population* and for the representative batch, a *sample*, though it is important not to take the word 'population' in this context to refer necessarily to a human group. Many data batches do refer to people, such as the population of users of a library service, but researchers are interested in many other important populations of tangible and intangible quantities, such as the number of books in a library, the number of requests for inter-library loans, number of citations of a particular reference, lengths of time spent online accessing a database and many many more.

It is highly unlikely that the data analyst will ever be working with population data, that is the collection of all data values referring to every case in the superbatch. Even where a population is well defined and documented, like the bookstock of a library, the population may be just too large to analyse in total. In many cases the superbatch of data values of interest is just not available, such as the times spent on different activities by various users during their visits to the library over a given period of time. It is necessary to work with sub-batches or samples of data from the large or, in some cases, potentially infinite target population of values of interest. Providing the batch is representative of the superbatch it is quite likely that nothing much is lost by working with a sample, in fact the results of analysis are quite likely to be much more accurate and reliable than if an attempt had been made to work with population data (Open University 1983, Unit A4).

A complete enumeration of all possible values in a superbatch is called a census, in contrast to a survey which aims to provide a representative sample batch for analysis. The important and interesting questions are: how can we tell whether any particular batch is representative of the whole population and how is one selected. The answer to the first question is that it is generally impossible to discover that a batch is precisely representative of the superbatch in its variable characteristics, but it is possible to determine how likely any particular batch represents the whole within calculable limits of accuracy. And the short answer to the second question is to choose a random sample.

The selection of a random sample is based upon ideas of

probability and some mathematical ideas which are not necessarily essential for the practising data analyst to be familiar with. The important principle to apply is that in selecting a random sample it is sufficient to ensure that every data value in the batch is chosen from the target population with a known probability of selection. In many cases the probabilities of selection are arranged to be exactly equal between all possible choices, but that is not strictly necessary to produce an analysable random sample and in many practical situations selection probabilities are arranged to be unequal for sound scientific reasons.

The batch of data in figure 6.1 is a sample of the sales of all softback titles published in Britain during 1988, but it is not a random sample, since it purposely presents those 100 titles with the greatest numbers of sales in 1988. It is not possible to apply statistical methods to estimate characteristics of the wider unknown superbatch with any known limits of confidence on the precision of the results. For all practical purposes it is probably sufficient to regard this batch as a population. If so, we can select a random sample from it and illustrate the way that population characteristics can be estimated from the sub-batch values.

Figures 6.12 and 6.13 show the result of selecting two random samples from figure 6.1, using the Minitab SAMPLE command.

```
MTB > print 'rank' 'nat' 'home' 'export'

ROW    rank    nat      home     export

  1       5      5    380083     240827
  2      53      2    123759      38483
  3      18      1    319980      47500
  4      58      5     68733      83484
  5      30      2     71856     198288
  6      29      2    179771     103698
  7      14      2    288891     151070
  8      92      2     75603      36372
  9      23      5    233914      74442
 10      69      2     97132      35901
 11      94      2     56423      55336
 12       6      3    391205     178472
 13      44      5     80457     105925
 14      82      2     84277      35026
 15      57      2    152667        223
 16      63      3     95816      50755
```

RAP(OU)

Fig. 6.12   Random sample from figure 6.1(16)

```
MTB > print 'rank' 'nat' 'home' 'export'

ROW    rank    nat     home     export

  1      88      2     91282     23188
  2      37      2    151932     56560
  3      52      5    110344     54909
  4      55      2    126860     28617
  5      68      2    125812     12667
  6      58      5     68733     83484
  7      15      2    360878     70241
  8      42      3    125392     74649
  9      44      5     80457    105925
```

RAP(OU)

Fig. 6.13 Random sample from figure 6.1(9)

Only four columns have been selected: 'rank' refers to the position of the title in the original list of top 100; 'nat' refers to the nationality of the author − 1 = Aus, 2 = Br, 3 = Ire, 4 = SA, 5 = US; plus 'home' and 'export' sales of titles.

Take a look at the characteristics of each sample using DES-CRIBE. Figure 6.14 shows the result for the sample of 16 first, then the sample of 9:

```
MTB > describe 'home' 'export'

                 N      MEAN    MEDIAN    TRMEAN     STDEV    SEMEAN
home            16    168785    110445    160924    116667     29167
export          16     89738     64889     85339     68723     17181

               MIN       MAX        Q1        Q3
home         56423    391205     76817    275147
export         223    240827     36900    139784




MTB > describe 'home' 'export'

                 N      MEAN    MEDIAN    TRMEAN     STDEV    SEMEAN
home             9    137966    125392    137966     87576     29192
export           9     56693     56560     56693     30618     10206

               MIN       MAX        Q1        Q3
home         68733    360878     85869    139396
export       12667    105925     25903     79066
```

RAP(OU)

Fig. 6.14 Summary commands for random samples

Compare the results to those for the population shown in figure 6.2. The sample estimates of the population values for the means and medians seem to be reasonably close; the estimates for the third quartile are not so close. Generally the estimates from the larger sample of 16 seem to be a little better than those from the smaller sample of 9.

Of course, if you take a sample of any size from a population you are not likely to get estimates of means and medians which are exactly equal to those of the population. Even if you select 90 out of a population of 100 there is a chance that there will be some sampling *error*. Of course there is also a small chance that even a fairly small sample like those above will provide exact estimates, but even if they did, how could we possibly know?

The answer to this is that, from the information available from the distribution of sample values, it is possible to estimate an interval for the population mean, median or quartiles etc., within which the population value is likely to lie, with a calculable degree of confidence expressed as a probability. Such an interval is called a *confidence interval* (CI) and, depending upon how wide it is, it might be referred to as a 90%, a 95% or 99% confidence interval indicating the probability with which the population value is likely to be contained within it.

Minitab can be used to provide quickly confidence intervals for the population mean or median estimated from random samples of different sizes. The principles underlying the procedures are covered by Open University (1983, Units B1,C2) and the use of Minitab by Ryan (1985).

From the sample of 16 a 95% confidence interval for the population median of home sales is (79,000–246,000); the actual value of 117,000 is included. A 95% CI for the mean is (107,000–231,000) which includes the actual mean 160,000. Figure 6.15 shows a Minitab boxplot for the sample of 16 values of home sales, with the position of the 95% CI for the population median indicated by parentheses within the box.

The sample of 9 does just about as well, the two CIs being (82,000–146,000) and (79,000–246,000) for the population median and mean respectively.

The 95% CIs might seem to be rather wide and of little practical use. In fact, they can be extremely useful in practical situations. A statistician bookseller with a bookstock consisting of several hundred titles was interested in ordering some plastic protective covers for all or as much of his stock as possible. The covers came in three sizes, at three different prices, and the problem was: how many of each size to order so as to keep costs

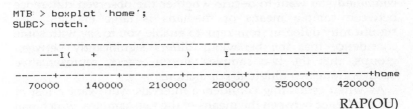

```
MTB > boxplot 'home';
SUBC> notch.

          ---------------------------
     ---I (      +            )      I--------------------
          ---------------------------
    ------+----------+----------+----------+----------+----------+home
      70000      140000     210000     280000     350000     420000
```

RAP(OU)

Fig. 6.15 Boxplot for 16 sample, home sales

as low as possible and yet provide covers for as many books as possible. A large book cannot be put into a smaller cover, but a small book can be put into a larger cover.

The solution to his problem lay in taking measurements of size from a suitably large sample from the total stock and from the sample estimating values, with CIs, for the median and quartiles of the total stock. This problem and its solution is analogous to the one facing a librarian who has to decide on how to arrange shelf heights in order to maximize the amount of storage space in a section of the library. A study describing this particular problem with alternative solutions, and different kinds of analysis, is reported in Chen (1978 pp. 63–5).

7. Testing for significance

Sometimes a particular research question is concerned not with estimating a confidence interval for a population value from the values in a sample, but in comparing two samples to see whether they might have come from the same population. For example, in a study of the frequency of reference by users to citation indexes, you might be interested to see whether there is any significant difference between different categories of user, say: men and women; final year students and postgraduates; science and social science students; daytime and evening users.

If you have random samples of data values for the variable of interest, corresponding to the different categories of user, you can estimate values for mean and median frequency of reference for the population of all users. If there is no significant difference between the behaviour patterns of the two subgroups, then the sample values will each provide estimates for the same overall population values. In that case, you would expect the average difference between sample means or sample medians to be zero, taken over a large number of different samples.

In practice you will usually only have a single sample for each category of user available and on the basis of the information contained you want to decide whether the observed difference between sample means or medians is large enough, i.e., significantly different from zero, to enable you to say with some confidence that the behaviour differs significantly between groups, that the two samples are, in effect, representative batches from two different populations.

As when estimating confidence intervals, you want a test of the difference between the means of the two samples, which will enable you to conclude with a known degree of confidence or probability that the underlying population means are significantly different at that level of confidence. It is usual, as before, to choose a 95% level of confidence, that is a probability level of significance of 5%, when making statements about the likely significance of the difference between two sample estimates of population values. It is not unusual to choose significance levels of 1% or 0.1%, corresponding to levels of confidence of 99% and 99.9%, depending upon the context and the research purpose.

There are many different kinds of significance test available depending upon whether the data is nominal, ordinal or interval/ratio and depending upon whether you are estimating proportions, medians, means, measures of spread or correlation or the adequacy of a straight line or curve as a fit to some time-series data, and so on.

The two samples taken from the 1988 softback sales dataset can be used to decide whether there is any significant difference between their estimates of the population mean level of home sales. The particular significance test used in this example is known as the 'two-sample t-test' which is computed by Minitab using the command TWOSAMPLE-T (or just TWOS) (Open University 1983, Unit C2, Ryan 1985 chapter 9).

Figure 6.16 displays the result of Minitab's TWOS for the means of the two samples of home sales. The symbol MU refers to an estimate of the mean of the common population from which it is assumed the two batches have been sampled. A 95% CI for the difference between the two estimates of the population mean runs from −55,000 to +116,000. Since this interval includes the value zero as an estimate of the difference, then it is possible to conclude with 95% confidence that there is no evidence from these two samples that they are batches from two different populations.

The t-test, TTEST, shows the result of testing the idea that the two samples provide estimates of equal population means against an alternative that the population means are not equal

```
MTB > twos 'home16' v 'home9'

TWOSAMPLE T FOR home16 VS home9
            N      MEAN     STDEV    SE MEAN
home16     16    168785    116667    29167
home9       9    137966     87576    29192

95 PCT CI FOR MU home16 - MU home9: (-55280, 116920)

TTEST MU home16 = MU home9 (VS NE): T= 0.75  P=0.46  DF=  20
```

RAP(OU)

Fig. 6.16 Two-sample t-test for random samples

(NE). The computed T value is 0.75 which has a P value, or probability, of 0.46. This can be interpreted as a result not significant at the 5% level (which would have a P value of 0.05). It is, perhaps, not surprising, and rather pleasing, that the result has turned out to confirm what we already know, that is that the two samples do, in fact, come from the same population.

Suppose, instead, that you want to compare home sales with export sales. Is there any evidence from the sample of 16 observations that the mean level of home sales in the population is significantly different from the mean level of export sales? Figure 6.17 displays the result of the Minitab TWOS to answer this question.

You can see that the 95% CI for the estimated difference in the population means runs from +9,000 to +148,000, which does not include zero, so there is evidence from this comparison that the population mean level of home sales is significantly different from the population mean level of export sales. The TTEST for the significance of the difference between the estimates of the two population means produces a value of T - 2.34 with a P value, or probability level, of 0.028 which is less than 5%.

```
MTB > twos 'home' v 'export'

TWOSAMPLE T FOR home VS export
            N      MEAN     STDEV    SE MEAN
home       16    168785    116667    29167
export     16     89738     68723    17181

95 PCT CI FOR MU home - MU export: (9166, 148929)

TTEST MU home = MU export (VS NE): T= 2.34  P=0.028  DF=  24
```

RAP(OU)

Fig. 6.17 Two-sample t-test for home v. export

So, it is possible to conclude that there is evidence on the basis of the sample of 16 data values for home sales and export sales, that there is a real difference between the overall population mean levels of home sales and export sales and that this difference is significant at the 5% level. Again this result is not surprising and confirms what we already know, that mean home sales are, in fact, much greater than mean export sales.

This short introduction to significance testing has done no more than scratch the surface of a vast and fascinating aspect of quantitative data analysis and research method. You should follow up your reading of this section and study of the two examples, with practice and further study based upon the texts referred to and using your own sample data.

8. More advanced methods

There is much more that could be said and must be done when considering the analysis of quantitative data, but this is not the place to pursue the topic much further. Instead of working with the raw data, or given numbers, collected during the research, it can be extremely useful, even necessary, to transform the values arithmetically before carrying out exploratory and confirmatory analysis. This might involve subtraction, multiplication or division of the data values or raising them to a power, taking the logarithms of values and so on. How and why you should do this is well described and exemplified by Marsh (1988 throughout, especially chapter 11).

More advanced methods are also concerned with teasing out and testing the significance of complex multiple relationships between sets of more than two variables. The complete set of techniques and skills associated with this is referred to as multivariate method. The mathematical modelling and statistical techniques of analysis associated with this can be complex and require a clear mind and a cool head. Computer data analysis programs can very easily produce results which are formidably difficult to make sense of. It is a good rule never to subject your data to any analysis unless you are sure beforehand that you have a strategy for interpreting the results in relationship to your substantive questions of research interest.

If you are coming to quantitative data analysis for the first time, and even if you are not, you should find that it is possible to do an immense amount of rewarding analysis based upon exploratory methods such as those using stemplots and scatterplots and two-way contingency tables. This can apply to the simultaneous modelling of more than two variables just as well as to the simpler situations. There is no one-way route to successful data analysis and there are rarely unique answers to research questions. The activity is just as much art as it is science.

9. References for further study and practice
For more complete coverage and development of the principles and techniques of data analysis outlined in this chapter, together with worked examples and plenty of practice exercises based upon a variety of real-world datasets, refer to one or more of the following:

Ehrenberg, A. S. C., *Data reduction: analysing and interpreting statistical data*, London, Wiley, 1975.

Marsh, C., *Exploring data: an introduction to data analysis for social scientists*, Cambridge, Polity, 1988.

Open University, *Statistics in society*, 16 volumes, Course MDST242, Milton Keynes, Open University Press, 1983.

Ryan, B. F., Joiner, T. A., and Ryan, T., *Minitab handbook*, 2nd edn, Boston, Duxbury, 1985.

Probably the single most useful, relevant and reliable reference to follow up is Marsh. To gain maximum benefit from a study of this book you should be able to work through all of the examples and exercises using the Minitab software package for data analysis and to do this you will need to refer to Ryan *et al.* and to the *Minitab reference manual*. The Open University Course, MDST242, like Marsh, adopts an approach based upon EDA (exploratory data analysis). In addition to the 16 volumes of text there are a number of audio and video cassettes in the Open University course, which are integral to its study. The book by Ehrenberg was published about ten years before any of the other references and therefore predates both EDA and the use of microcomputers for data analysis. Nevertheless, it is an extremely valuable companion to the later works and could very usefully be studied in isolation.

A useful reference to quantitative data analysis in library studies is: Chen, Ching-chih, *Quantitative measurement and dynamic library service*, London, Mansell, Oryx, 1978. This source also predates EDA and the use of data analysis software on personal computers, but it does provide some useful illustrations of some data analysis techniques in library contexts.

Minitab is a registered trademark of Minitab, Inc.
Lotus 1-2-3 is a registered trademark of Lotus Development Corporation.

DBase IV is a registered trademark of Ashton Tate.
Open University course materials, text and AV, are available
from: Open University Educational Enterprises Ltd
        12 Cofferidge Close
        Stony Stratford
        Milton Keynes MK11 1BY.

7 Qualitative research

Margaret Slater

1. The subjective-objective research spectrum

All social research and indeed much that is designated as scientific research, has qualitative aspects and subjective elements. Unless researchers recognize, accept and admit that, they render the research process itself vulnerable, open to criticism as unscientific, as pseudo-quantitation, as misleading attempts to measure the unmeasurable.

Take the physical sciences. Consider the very choice of which factors to include and which to exclude in designing a controlled experiment. This decision is an exercise in informed, but still ultimately subjective, human judgement. In the life sciences, medical research may involve careful observation and defined measurement of pulse and respiration rate and blood pressure. Yet the fact that the objects of study are human beings introduces some uncontrollable and qualitative elements. Some people get nervous about having their blood pressure taken. So it goes up. Others remain unperturbed. Contextual factors also impinge. On any particular day, a patient may have good cause to feel worried, depressed, or conversely, euphoric. So mood, as well as physical state, may affect readings and tests. Patients' feelings about researchers conducting tests (liked or disliked) may affect results. Medical researchers are not necessarily naive. Yet even if they are aware of the totality of these complex sources of bias, how on earth are they going to make allowances for or to weight all of them? In addition, some of their material is gathered perforce in qualitative mode, in the form of patient descriptions of symptoms, side-effects and pain levels. These are described by people with different personal vocabularies, different pain thresholds, and different psychological degrees of stoicism. What one person calls agony, another may call pain, or even discomfort, or more picturesquely sum up in metaphorical terms as feeling under the weather, totally rotten, or even 'wishing I was dead'.

How much more so is this the case in social research, where the very field of study is concerned with the behaviour patterns of, and interaction between human beings, or between human beings and systems, objects or animals? Thus social research, and in particular that branch of it known as qualitative research, is very open to accusation of manufacturing a mystique to mask mere mumbo-jumbo and undisciplined charlatanry. Social researchers must be constantly prepared to explain and defend the use and legitimacy of qualitative methods of enquiry. The very real difference between what Peter Reason has called unacceptably 'naive research' and 'critical subjectivity' needs to be spelled out.[29]

As a respondent said in a recent survey I did amongst social scientists:

I don't actually personally believe that you can attain complete objectivity. But I don't believe the natural sciences do either, inasmuch as they are bound by their historical and social contexts. Scientific theories are, you know, true for their own time, putting it very crudely. This is true for natural sciences, and it's certainly true for social sciences. Having said that, I don't think it's a case against social science. It's just in the nature of human beings studying each other, and I think it's possible to undertake very rigorous social investigation and come up with valid information about the world from it.

Hopefully, by the end of this chapter, it will have been demonstrated that the qualitative research position is tenable. If this aim has not been achieved entirely, perhaps dubious opponents may at least be prepared to think more open-mindedly about the advantages, as well as the drawbacks, of the qualitative approach.

2. Qualitative and quantitative social research
So, all social research, and indeed other kinds of research, involuntarily and unavoidably embrace some qualitative elements. Within social research itself, however, there are two schools of thought, methodology and practice, called quantitative research and qualitative research. It is with this kind of qualitative/quantitative research dichotomy that we are now concerned. Because this is the age of the specialist, researchers tend to get typecast, promoting and practising the philosophy and methodology of one or the other school.

Research users and funders, according to their past experience and natural bent, may also prefer to commission a quantitative rather than a qualitative study, or vice versa. Client reasons for doing so are not always or necessarily rational, nor dictated by the nature of the problem requiring study. What do we mean then, when we talk about qualitative and quantitative work within the area of social research itself? What dictates the use of one methodology rather than the other? Certainly, method and subject of enquiry need to be in harmony, not conflict, to obtain optimal information and insight. But is it always and inevitably a matter of circumstance dependent, mutually exclusive choice? Or should, ideally, the two approaches be used in a compensatory way to study almost any problem or phenomenon – although probably in different proportions of qualitative to quantitative ingredients in different cases, and with sensitive application of either method to appropriate aspects of the topic under exploration?

This chapter (a) explores possible answers to these questions, (b) broadly and briefly describes the aims and some of the techniques of qualitative research, (c) outlines some advantages and disadvantages of the qualitative approach, in terms of different purposes and problems. Where relevant, it draws on actual qualitative research experience.

2.1 *Quantitative research*
Let's begin by negative definition, by looking at what qualitative research is not. So let's quickly examine its alleged antithesis, quantitative research. Typically, this involves counting or measuring – the application of subsequent statistical tests to results in order to detect or confirm trends. The data-collecting instrument (often but not invariably a questionnaire), must be pre-tested and standardized to produce reliable results, and to screen out as much systematic and random bias as is humanly possible. The aim is to get clear-cut, precise, accurate results that factually reflect the situation under study.

Quantitative research, as its name implies, tends to deal in mass data. The greater the number of cases studied, within reason and observing the law of diminishing returns, the more accurate this picture of wider reality is likely to be – provided that the numerous cases included are representative of the relevant parent population from which they are drawn. Techniques used to collect data from the sample involve rigorous standardization of the content, phrasing and administration of the survey instrument, say, the questionnaire. Questions and answers occur within controlled frameworks – e.g., of fixed options to be selected from pre-supplied answer categories, the most extreme case being 'answer yes or no'. Quantitative research thus produces a lucid, and apparently or hopefully objective description of the subject of study. Counting and measuring are involved: so the whole approach seems to have something in common with scientific method.

This approach can be fine, if you already know quite a bit about your subject. Say that you know a certain phenomenon occurs, and what that phenomenon is, but you need to know how often it happens and to what kind of people in demographic terms. What, however, if you do not fully understand the nature of the phenomenon, and you have not a clue why or how it happens? In this case you will be unable to provide respondents with sensible, meaningful lists of precoded answer alternatives. Or what if the complexity of the topic cannot be reduced to simple yes/no responses? In such situations, qualitative methods apply and can help discover what is really going on.

If you want to measure how often something happens, and describe its occurrence in very strictly controlled terms, then the quantitative approach will suit your project. If, on the other hand, you are interested in the detailed structure and nature of what is happening, and above all in why, then qualitative research will give a richer answer, more informative material and more insight. It is concerned with the nature of the phenomenon under study rather than its incidence in statistical terms, also with its subjective experience by respondents. As its name implies, it seeks the essence or quality of experience. It also fruitfully explores causation.

2.2 *Qualitative research*
Qualitative research makes different and often heavier demands on researcher and respondent in terms of time and effort. So you can be into what is sometimes called a non-sampling situation at the inception. Frequently you cannot count or test the findings obtained at the conclusion. Cost, time and interviewer fatigue preclude going out to a sample of epic proportions. Funds are being invested in depth and detail, not in breadth. Typically you might interview in depth a limited number of individual respondents. The number will depend on the job itself and financial, manpower and deadline constraints. Useful qualitative work can be done with as few as 20 interviews. A sample of 200 would be a big one, these days, in this field of activity. Or you might decide to hold half a dozen group discussions, which could expose you to the experience and attitudes of up to 60 people.

The normal, rigorous, statistical rules of sampling may be inapplicable to recruiting participants. Nevertheless, the principles still apply as guidelines to procedure. It is important not to gather together a highly atypical or biased bunch of people. A worst case example might be the friends, neighbours, relations, or immediate colleagues of a lazy, or overworked interviewer or recruiter. Incidentally, if you are delegating recruiting to others, it is vital not to ask the impossible of them. Simple consideration, not asking others to do anything you yourself would be unwilling to attempt, or incapable of carrying out, should suffice as a rule of thumb. If interviewers or recruiters 'cheat', suspect an unrealistically demanding brief as the prime cause. Given the choice, most people prefer to do an honest day's work.

Many think of qualitative research mainly in terms of depth interviews and group discussions. Certainly, these are heavily relied upon. They are what you might call the bread and butter techniques. In actuality, however, as Mary Goodyear pointed out: 'Qualitative research is a many-splendoured thing and certain problems and clients will respond to one type of approach, whilst other problems and other clients need to be offered something else. There is no one correct way to do qualitative research. It all depends on your problem.'[10]

In discussing the contribution of qualitative research to social policy, Jane Ritchie identified five categories of purpose or aim, each relating to a different research question.[30]

1. Contextual or descriptive research: What's going on here?
2. Diagnostic research: Why does it exist or happen?
3. Evaluation research: How well does it happen or exist?
4. Strategic research: What (if anything) should be done about it?
5. Contribution to research theory: generation of theoretical statements, at one level or another, about the social world.

A single piece of qualitative research might well cover more than one of the above areas at once – e.g., what and why. Probably it could not cover all aspects at once. Evaluation of the process under study as beneficial or malign, and then any strategic research, might well be separate stages carried out after digestion of what and why findings. Descriptive or contextual research might stand in for strategic research, by informing and guiding policy makers, so that they felt competent to make decisions. As Jane Ritchie says: 'A significant element of the contribution qualitative methods can make is in *enlightening* policy makers about the lives and experiences of those for whom policy is formulated.'[30] That statement has considerable relevance to the value of qualitative user studies in our own field, and to library policies and rules that affect users.

3. Questionnaires, interviews and group discussions

In considering methodology, let's start with the admittedly obvious, with questionnaires, interview surveys and group discussions. It is in this area that the complementarity of qualitative and quantitative research is most clearly demonstrated. A highly structured questionnaire for mass distribution and self-completion will benefit greatly if it is based on the findings of preliminary qualitative work. Probably this would be done by face-to-face interviewing, perhaps by group discussion. Such foundation work will, at the least, provide the designer of the subsequent quantitative questionnaire with the natural language and concepts used by respondents when discussing the topic of the survey. So the resulting structured questionnaire will be easy for people to complete. It will make sense to them, being readily comprehensible and unambiguous. It will not force them into false and artificial choices between sundry researcher pre-conceptions and misconceptions, expressed in alien (and often alienating) language. Material obtained will be more genuinely representative of its suppliers. Response rate may even be higher.

As an extra fail-safe device, it is good practice to include an 'other answer, please explain' option, at the end of pre-set answer lists in the structured questionnaires of quantitative research. In fact, this other answer alternative is a micro-qualitative question, in form and content. Similarly, at the end of a mass quantitative survey, when the data has been collected and analysed, qualitative research may subsequently be used. Interviewing or group discussions could help at this stage to clarify unexpected ambiguities of response or odd combinations of response revealed by cross-analysis.

Handling of discussions and interviews will be dealt with in some detail in chapter 8. In this more general and introductory chapter it may be more profitable to consider the circumstances in which you might use one method rather than the other. Techniques and results obtained are somewhat different. Discussions and interviews are not perfect substitutional alternatives. The outcome differs and the role of the interviewer and group discussion facilitator are different, for good reasons inherent in the basic nature of the two events.

Group discussions can be helpful when total time expenditure and funds are restricted, also when fairly rapid input to the study is needed. Practical considerations of this sort may considerably influence choice between the two methods. Some researchers claim that the kind of client commissioning the research can dictate such choice (unless the researcher uses counter-pressure, client education and persuasive argument). Allegedly, commercial enterprises and advertising agencies are much more likely to agree to, or positively want, groups as the information gathering medium. Perhaps this is just because they wanted the results yesterday? But maybe they are relatively research sophisticated, and understand that group discussions do fit certain research problems rather well, particularly the kind of problems they themselves possess. Clients from the non-profit sector, for instance policy makers at central and local government levels, are said to be inclined to favour interview studies. Such clients seem to believe that research conducted by interview is somehow more respectable, profound, even more scientific, than that based on group discussions.

Of course it is not true that the group method is just a slick, corner-cutting gimmick deployed by cowboys. If you feel that your topic will be best studied by working with groups of respondents, it is up to you, in all integrity, to convince your funder that this is the case. On the other hand, if the balance of advantage between group and individual interview is virtually indiscernible, it may be well to remember that conservative clients reputedly find interviews more acceptable, and so may be prepared to pay for them if they cost more than groups.

Yet the real difference between groups and interviews is not a matter of cost and client preference. It concerns results and applications. It is indicated by name. Groups are not called discussions idly. They are *not* group interviews. At group discussions interplay occurs on a variety of levels – social, verbal, intellectual, emotional, attitudinal. Themes emerge and are developed participatively and freely (within reasonable limits of the defined topic) in and by a group of people, in *discussion*. Groups are thus characterized by breadth of free-ranging exploration. But depth of individual reaction and experience are sacrificed to obtain this varied input. If you need to go deeply and in detail into the experiences and reactions of respondents you would do better to research by interview (or possibly in some circumstances collect case histories in some other way, for example, diary-keeping or self-taping).

Qualitative interviews span a spectrum from operation within a relatively structured framework to the free interview. At the tight end of the scale is the administration by an interviewer of a fixed wording, fixed order questionnaire. Responses to its questions, however, will be mainly open-ended, recorded verbatim in the respondent's own words. At the loose end of the scale, the interviewer may only have a list of topics to be covered within the interview. The respondent is allowed, in fact encouraged, to talk freely and expansively on the main subject, raising topics within it in any order s/he wishes. Letting the respondent take overt control in this way can be very productive. The order in which sub-topics are raised spontaneously can indicate priorities and association of ideas. Failure to mention a topic at all may be significant. In the classic depth interview, apart from reminding the respondent that he or she is still interested, the interviewer tries not to intervene much, until the final mopping up stage. Only then will the interviewer explore the hidden agenda points that the respondent has not covered. Questions put by the interviewer at this (and indeed at any) stage should be recorded. A transcript of a depth interview that reads like a monologue will be very misleading to the person who has to analyse it.

The more fully and accurately any interview can be recorded in the respondent's own words, the better analysis and conclusions will be. So a tape-recorder can be a useful aid, but has a few drawbacks that may not be immediately obvious to those who have not used one in this context. Not least of these problems are subsequent time investment and labour costs of transcription. If you have no time and money to transcribe tapes, you may end up with a lot of marvellous material locked up in the tapes, virtually inaccessible, except in a dipstick, impressionistic way.

Of course the tape-recorder is liberating from the constraint of constant scribbling and the artificiality and slow pace that this imposes on the interview. The whole affair becomes more like an ordinary conversation with normal eye contact. But this can make the respondent very aware that you are contributing nothing but vague interjections. Rapport can evaporate. The temptation to the inexperienced interviewer to talk, to play a part in this 'conversation', can be tremendous.

Perhaps part of this problem is that the stock in trade verbal encouragements of the depth interviewer would, as normal conversational gambits, signal boredom – the typical contributions of a bored or boring person. Such non-directive probes include: 'mm', 'uh-huh', 'tell me more about that', 'why's that', 'what makes you feel that way', and of course playback of the respondent's last words. A succinct comment on such techniques that I once heard was: 'But who wants a parrot for a friend?' The real point about your role as interviewer, however, which you must somehow get over to the respondent, is that although friendly, you are not a friend, in the accepted sense of the word. You are an interested listener, the perfect ear. You have a sincere, non-judgemental interest in anything they care to and can tell you on the topic in question. But it is not your place to influence nor advise them (as a friend might do).

The classic received wisdom on interviewing has been outlined above. The modern researcher, however, should also be aware and try to evaluate the growing popularity of the school of interviewing known as 'dialogic research'. Interviewer and respondent here engage in a genuine dialogue and mutually explore the survey topic.[29] This method transcends the artificiality and rapport loss experienced in passive interviewing of professional and expert respondents, who don't suffer fools gladly, and may mistake the classic depth interviewer for a simpleton. Even worse, they may see through the whole stratagem and resent being taken for a fool, and manipulated. Because of its natural suitability to such interviewing and hence to library-information research, the reader is urged to explore this philosophy. Do some background reading in this area and assess dialogic research merits for yourself and your purposes.

Considering purpose, solo interviews have a reputation of being better media than group discussions for exploring sensitive or confidential issues. Examples of such danger zones in the library-information field might be budgets and salaries, organizational status, the professional stereotype, relations with users, staff, higher management, or librarians versus information managers or scientists. Yet this can depend on just what is the delicate issue. To take an example outside our field, parents may be relieved, and talk as freely at a group discussion as they would at an interview, about problems in raising and educating children. The fact that other group members, complete strangers, also experience problems is reassuring and relaxing. Similarly, library managers may discuss problems with staff, users, higher management, with great freedom in a group, once it gets going. They will certainly listen with interest to any member of the group who claims to have encountered a particular problem and solved it.

In this context of delicate issues, it is worth pondering the perceived neutrality of library-information researchers investigating library matters. Inhouse research raises this problem in a pungent form. Contracting out of conduct of interviews or discussions to neutrals, (other) social researchers, should ideally be considered, when studying topics that may involve respondent criticism of the library-information community itself. If you can't afford this, which is highly likely in inhouse research, at least be aware that some respondents may have been inhibited by politeness, been less than frank in answers. Such statements do not necessarily imply that library-information researchers are incapable of proper, impartial conduct of such research. They do imply that respondents may be constrained in their presence.

To sum up: qualitative research, by interview or discussion, has a role not only in mapping or defining the nature of the research problem, but particularly in investigating its more sensitive aspects. Its role is not just that of adjunct to quantitative research. It is a major research mode in its own right. In general, if you want social interaction and a range of responses revealed, use group discussions. If you want to go deeply into case histories, individual reactions and motivation, use interviews.

4. Telephone research: qualitative aspects

Telephone interviewing is a relatively new aspect of survey work, well established in the United States, and on the increase in the United Kingdom. It offers a very cost and time-effective way of contacting large and geographically spread samples, particularly when CATI systems are used (Computer Aided Telephone Interviewing). Now most people will assert that telephone interviewing is necessarily quantitative research. They will stress that the questionnaire schedule must be short, simple, readily comprehensible and adhered to scrupulously. Personally, I have found that the exact opposite can be true. Consequently, I believe that telephone, like any other kind of interviewing, can be quantitative or qualitative, as the topic demands and interviewing skills permit. Telephone interviews to which I have been subjected, as respondent, were not good by the standards of quantitative research to which they, presumably, aspired. These interviews were superficial and constraining. It was difficult to say what I really thought and had experienced. No pre-codes ever seemed to exist to fit my case and interviewers were manifestly disinterested in other answers. On conclusion, one felt irritated, cheated. Somehow one had been lured into agreement with ideas and behaviour that were not one's own, for ill-defined purposes. Obviously, the telephone is not a natural winner as a vehicle for any and every kind of quantitative research (e.g. the more complex, where ideally, you might wish to make things easier for respondents by using show-cards).

Yet ten years ago, when surveying manpower planning and forecasting practices in the United Kingdom, I did the bulk of the study by free interview over the telephone. This involved cold contact by telephone with high level manpower planning experts in fields other than library-information work, like pharmacy, medicine, teaching, engineering, civil aviation. From these people I had to find out what problems and techniques they had, of possible relevance to manpower forecasting for the information workforce of the future.

Quickly, I discovered for myself what the telephone interviewing experts will rightly tell you. Namely, that the first 30 seconds are crucial to establishing credibility, topic definition, and some sort of rapport. After that, it was relatively plain sailing, if not always absolutely easy. In fact, a strange rapport developed, in which two disembodied intelligences, sharing a mutual interest, communicated quite spontaneously. In doing so, they were undistracted by appearance, physical mannerisms, age, surroundings and the other incidentals that can influence a face-to-face interview. Some respondents were so interested that they invited me round later 'to continue the discussion', or suggested that I join groups they belonged to, like the Manpower Society. Response rate I found literally incredible. Nobody refused to talk to me. Nobody hung up on me (or quickly terminated proceedings more politely). In short, I found the telephone an excellent medium for a long interview in depth, of loose structure, on a complex topic.[33]

As telephone interviewing adepts emphasize, it was necessary to compensate for the non-visual nature of the exchange, by more verbal input or simple noise, than in a face-to-face interview. Constant reminder by sound alone that you are still there and still interested is important. It also helped to have a well-defined field of enquiry that could be introduced with the minimum of verbiage and quickly understood by the listener. Relevance was immediately obvious. So there were no 'why pick on me' or 'what's this got to do with me' skirmishes at the outset. Professor Moore's advice to researchers, that they must be capable if required of summing up the aim of their study in a single sentence, may be exemplified here (see chapter 1).

Long free interviews by telephone may be more practicable when dealing with professional respondents at work than with members of the public at home. One atypical feature of this survey was that as the interview progressed, I was able to feed in more information and input than usual. A two-way dialogic transaction was necessary, with explanation of the state of play in the library-information field regarding manpower statistics and forecasting. This free interchange and interactive discussion helped rapport. People I telephoned also tended kindly to assume that I was a fellow forecaster, or to forget that basically I was a researcher. At the time I was well into the manpower field. I knew the journals, jargon and theory. So I was able to sustain this illusion of expertise without confessing alienating ignorance every few minutes. In this respect, the study had much in common with participant observation, but without the observation itself.

5. Non-verbal behaviour as research data

Now we seem to be sliding naturally here, from discussion of verbal communication, towards non-verbal communication and the allied area of observation, as an aspect of qualitative research. Non-verbal behaviour amounts to information given off, as opposed to information given, as in verbal communication. The good qualitative interviewer should always be alert to visual evidence and sensitive to body language as a two-way communication process. At least two reasons exist for that statement. The first concerns establishment and monitoring of rapport. The second involves noting behavioural clues relevant to the topic under study. An obvious example of the latter is actual behaviour that contradicts or belies what the respondent is saying, the self-reported behaviour.

A social researcher reported an illustrative anecdote about interviewing a librarian on user needs and user relations. The librarian was holding forth about the importance of instant and empathetic response to user demands. The interviewer was suitably impressed, until an actual user suddenly bumbled into the office doorway, tentatively asking: 'I'm sorry to interrupt, but I can't find anyone else. Can you help me look something up in the catalogue?' 'Look, can you come back later', snapped the librarian, 'I'm right in the middle of an important meeting here and I can't stop now.' The user retired, red-faced and apologetic, maybe never to return. The point of this story is that the interviewer who stuck rigidly to schedule, ignored and did not record this impromptu exchange, would be losing some rich and enlightening observational material, in which words and actions were inextricably mixed. The conclusion the researcher might reach, faced with recurrence of such observational evidence, is that it is easier to have the right professional philosophy than it is to live up to it.

To return to rapport and non-verbal clues to intensity and nature of feeling. Guidelines by Forbes and Jackson[8] state:

> Positive non-verbal behaviour involves doing friendly things like smiling, head-nodding and looking directly at others. . . . Negative non-verbal behaviour communicates difficulty or dislike by means of frowning, avoiding any eye contact, and letting the eyes wander.

Painfully obvious advice, perhaps, but worth while, because it is amazingly easy to forget what *you* are doing while interviewing. Forbes and Jackson also comment on behavioural echo, imitation of posture or gesture when intellectual or emotional agreement or liking occur. So interviewers must watch what they themselves are doing, as well as watching the respondent. Otherwise something may be projected to the respondent that may bias or damage the interview.

Fenton[7] and Kazlauskas[18] who have independently studied non-verbal communication in libraries, make some interesting points about body language. Fenton says that 'in gross terms, symmetrical postures correlate with tenseness and asymmetrical postures with relaxation and feeling at ease.' More manifest signs of feeling uneasy include 'scratching, hand-wringing, seam-straightening and cuff-fingering'. Such signals call for interviewer reassurance. Kazlauskas also points out the significance of sitting and standing in interview situations. It is no accident, he says, that we talk about sitting in judgement and standing trial. Relative status is positionally symbolized. Yet the sitting-standing power balance is fluid and context-determined. After all, we also talk about standing over someone and brow-beating them. The moral is to be aware of current significance. Don't put yourself in a dominant position in an interview by sitting or standing at inappropriate times. Aim for equality: stand when your informants do; sit when they sit.

6. Observational studies

Observation, or man-watching as Desmond Morris calls it, thus plays an important incidental part in qualitative research.[24] Broader-based and more systematic observation can also be the main technique in its own right. Experts debate whether this is ever a completely neutral voyage of discovery, and if so whether and to what degree it should be theory laden before embarkation. Observation can also be carried out in controlled or 'laboratory' conditions, or in decontrolled and natural circumstances. An excellent illustration of the two modes is provided by Professor Henry Wynn.[36] He cites the example of a football manager who wishes to test the skills of a number of aspirants to his/her team.

Although the various skills (heading, passing, etc.) can be tested in a controlled way, the players' eventual success must also depend on the extent to which these skills are required in an actual football match. Thus, in some sense another experiment at a different level (of observation) is needed to study the frequency of use of skills.

Observational technique can range from covert neutral watching to participant observation. In covert man-watching, the researcher adopts an 'I am a camera' stance. Perhaps the researcher just sits in a library all day, observing and noting what goes on. No one will pay much attention to this apparent reader, who is not participating in nor influencing what happens. At the other end of the observational scale is full participant observation. Here the observer infiltrates the action, playing some role which permits him or her to do so. Perhaps the role is that of an active user, asking certain questions, or behaving in certain ways. Or perhaps the observer joins the library staff. Interaction is inevitable. Thus the reality studied is influenced. The researcher may also lose detachment and objectivity over time. To compensate, deeper insight into processes will be gained. Covert observers see mostly surfaces. Deducing what lies beneath is as subjective as immersion in it, although in a different way. Attempts at super-scientific observation may merely gather superficial data and come to superficial conclusions.

Some experts think that participant observers should avoid, or at least minimize, perturbation of the very situation they seek to explore. A lofty ideal, but somewhat impractical. Maybe this is why others believe that it is legitimate to give reality a helping nudge, just to see what happens (particularly in stalemate situations).

Some degree of influence seems unavoidable in participant observation. Complete neutrality when role playing would make the researcher highly conspicuous. So accept that you have influenced reality. Try, however, to note and record when, where, how and why this happened. This leads to consideration of recording observations in general. It simply is not possible to watch and record everything. Perception is selective. Not everything that happens will have relevance to the research aims and hypothesis. Even if you could watch everything, you would certainly have problems in analysing the resulting mass of data. Systematization of observation and recording is necessary, otherwise analysis will be very difficult. A daily log for recording observations might be a good idea. This log could be sequential, a chronological record of the day's significant events. Or it could be categorized under headings, a classified log in effect. If sequential, at some stage of analysis you will need to categorize and regroup material, so that you can discern behavioural trends. If you are not very familiar with the subject under study, a loose initial approach might be necessary, because you do not yet know enough to categorize with assurance. The subject of observation is covered in detail in chapter 9.

7. The qualitative report: analysis and presentation of findings
Analysis of qualitative material is discussed fully in chapter 8. Reporting in general is the subject of chapter 10. Nevertheless, brief composite overview may have value here. Analytical principles and procedures, and the kind of report emerging from a qualitative study, usually differ greatly from those of a quantitative one. Of course, information reduction, synthesis and trend plotting are needed, as in a quantitative project. It would be a ludicrous exercise to try to compress and express the results of depth interviews amongst 20 people, in a series of numerical tables. Yet it might be relevant to state textually that about two-thirds, or all, or none of these respondents had visited a bookshop or used a library in the past year. At the same time, you must be aware that you cannot extrapolate from this finding to any wider population, as you would be able to do in a quantitative study of a large sample. To detect trends and patterns in the case of unstructured interview material, you might find it useful to construct an interview summary for each respondent, systematizing and categorizing the content.

Ideally, a qualitative report should give the feel and flavour of the situation studied, in depth. This calls for sensitive interpretation of information collected, and creative presentational skills, in order to communicate findings. Quotations from actual interviews and discussions, of observational descriptions and case history material aid immediacy and reader comprehension. They also play fair with readers, by showing them typical evidence on which your interpretation is based. To play fair with your respondents, however, you must always make any such citation anonymous. Participants must not be identified or identifiable.

Verbatim material from respondents will require content

analysis. If it results from fixed-wording, open-ended questions, you should be able to identify and code recurrent answer categories, key concepts and behaviour patterns. If the sample is large and representative enough, you may be able to count them, cross-analyse them by answers to other (probably more factual or demographic) questions. You may even be able to test the results of such cross-sorts for significance. Much depends on the pattern-discerning skill and consistency of the designer of the coding schedule and of the actual coder of answers.

Unstructured depth interviews could be coded in this way, for analyst convenience. So could group discussions. But because this kind of questioning cannot be rigorously controlled, sequenced and standardized, it is not safe to take any counts of responses very seriously. In a group discussion, for instance, one person may raise a topic, two or three more may debate it. You don't always know what the rest think. You don't even know if this topic would have arisen at all if the first person had not introduced it. Focused summaries of the content of discussions and interviews may, nevertheless, considerably aid the analysis process, although they will not generate data safely expressable in numerical terms. From such summaries you may be able to construct master charts, summarizing the key concepts emerging from the entire study.

8. Content analysis
Content analysis can also be applied to very different material. So far, I have concentrated on active information gathering, by interview, discussion, or by man-watching. In qualitative research, however, one should not neglect *objets trouvés*, ready-made material existing to hand. Documents and records, published and unpublished, can be subjected to content analysis. Typically, this would seem to be the modus operandi of the historical researcher, but it has its place in social research. Researchers in the information field – e.g. Nick Moore and Blaise Cronin – have analysed job advertisements.[5, 22] Thereby they learned a lot about employer perceptions and expectations of library-information workers. Cronin also analysed university and polytechnic prospectuses in relation to the content and slant of library-information courses in the UK.[5] Both curriculum vitae and organization charts were subjected to analysis in a study of career patterns, job mobility and the occupational image.[32]

Social researchers have analysed entries in *Who's who*, short stories in popular magazines, advertisements for various products, in endeavours to learn more about changing perspectives in society over time.

Diaries and respondent-compiled case histories can also be content analysed. These may or may not fall into the category of *objets trouvés*. Perhaps they existed already: perhaps they were constructed at the request of the researcher. If the latter, they will be more focused, containing less redundancy and hopefully easier to analyse. All diaries and respondent-supplied case histories really amount to recorded self-observation. They will have been subjected to some systematization and editing by their creators, at the conscious and/or unconscious level.

9. Games and tests

Finally let us consider an aspect of qualitative research which amounts to inviting respondents to play games.[11] A vast battery of oblique information-gathering techniques exists in this area. It includes role playing, drawing pictures, telling stories, arranging show-cards in ways meaningful to respondents, responding to projective pictures, imagining what one might do in hypothetical situations, or completing sentences like: 'librarians are often . . .' or 'one thing I really dislike about libraries is . . .'.

The outcome of such grown-up games can sometimes be put through quite stringent analysis – e.g., the grouping of a fixed number of show-cards. Systematic attitude measurement comes into this category. The respondent is operating in subjective mode, dealing with his or her own feelings or reactions, when the question is answered. The researcher tackles the material supplied in vigorous reductionist mode. Often results are presented in the form of plotted charts. Visual similarity with experimental results in the physical or life sciences is evident. Thus the respondent's task is qualitative, but the results the researcher gets resemble those of a quantitative test and can be handled and presented as such.[14, 25]

Other products of such games, however, like respondents' art work, can be remarkably difficult to analyse, even by skilled and experienced researchers. So the analyst might think: 'Now this male librarian in this picture here looks a pretty ugly customer to me. Looks like a gorilla with a hangover.' But what is the respondent's standard of beauty? (And what is the analyst's?) How well can this respondent communicate concepts of beauty or ugliness, given the level of artistic skill at his or her personal disposal? Maybe the respondent meant to draw a well-built librarian (not effete, not a wimp), of at least average attractiveness of appearance and pleasantness of disposition.

Unless you ask such a respondent to describe in words what

he or she has drawn for you (which might be alienating or downright insulting), you just don't know the answers to the above questions, in any one individual case. Certainly, patterns might emerge over a large sample of drawings, particularly if control or comparison groups of drawings of members of other occupations were included. Incidentally, in the context of use of artwork, you can collect and use published cartoons as raw material, for example when studying the image of the profession.

All these esoteric techniques are great fun for researchers and for some – but by no means all – respondents. One defect of projective and allied methods is that not all grown-ups like playing games, particularly not for the ill-defined benefit of a relative stranger. Game or role playing may appeal to the frivolous, the self-assured, the relaxed, the fun-loving, the creative and the lateral thinkers. Serious-minded people, or highly logical thinkers, rationalists, or people with a strong sense of their own importance, or a low sense of security, or simply lacking in a sense of humour, may find such tests either silly, or deeply offensive. So they may refuse to attempt them, or even break off an interview at that point. They could feel that their intelligence, and the importance of the subject of enquiry, have been insulted or trivialized by such a childish manipulative task.

Consequently, response rate can be low and material gathered from such tests unrepresentative of the total population under scrutiny. A cartoon in a careers survey[32] showed a child asking its parents if it could be a librarian when it grew up. A blank balloon was supplied in the drawing, inviting respondents to supply the parental response. The responses were illuminating and easily subjected to content analysis. Common themes recurred with regularity. It drew, however, a lower response rate than any other question in the survey. Some people did not attempt it. Others objected and said why. Other literal minded people said: 'I can't answer this because I'm not a parent. But if a friend's child asked me that, I'd say do (or don't) because . . .'. That was in fact a perfectly acceptable response. Yet its form indicates the problems some respondents have with projective techniques.

Why bother to use such techniques at all then? Why play dangerous games with respondents, who may feel that if you ask a silly question, you deserve a silly answer? One good reason is that people often find it easier to externalize their own feelings, beliefs, attitudes, projectively onto an imaginary person, or into a hypothetical situation. All such specific tests, however, need to be scrutinized to remove biasing or totally irrelevant detail. Otherwise respondents may seize upon such false cues as significant items, thus unwittingly confusing the issue. Careful pretesting for general validity and reliability are also necessary.

To reduce difficulty of interpretation, it can sometimes be oddly effective to dispense with graphic interview aids. Instead you can use verbal ones. You can paint word pictures and ask respondents to reply in the same mode. Remember that minimalistic restraint is the key here. Aim at expression or *communication minceur*. Select exactly the right words with care. Avoid unnecessary verbiage. Redundant words are like unnecessary detail in pictures and may be equally misleading, increasing the possibility of errors of interpretation.

The technique of verbal portraiture can be used successfully in a self-completed questionnaire. For example, participants were asked in a mail survey to 'describe a typical librarian' and then to 'describe an ideal librarian'.[34] Results were amenable to systematic analysis. Contrasts between perceived actuality and the ideal librarian were particularly enlightening. Respondents did not seem to object to this approach, although some obviously found the task easier than others, so they were more forthcoming and detailed in their replies. When you ask questions like this, you may find that some answers are deadly serious, thoughtful and analytical in tone. Others may be more lighthearted, sometimes quite deliberately funny. At first this tonal variation can be worrying. Can such responses be thrown into the same reductive melting pot as the more serious answers? In this particular survey,[34] answers were coded as serious, frivolous, and neutral or indeterminate. The interesting thing was that when the conceptual content of these three answer categories was analysed, the same themes emerged in similar proportions. This was not a one-off event. Analyses in this dimension in other surveys since have produced similar results. As Freud pointed out, a long time ago and rather more elegantly, in *The psychopathology of everyday life*, many a true word is spoken in jest.

The most brilliant use of the verbal portrait technique in the library-information field that I can recall was the snapshot question employed by Bob Sergean in the Sheffield Manpower Project.[31] This study explored the nature of library-information work and the skills it required. Sergean asked respondents: 'Suppose you had to suggest a typical "snapshot" of yourself at work to illustrate the nature of your job. What would it show you doing?' The kind of illuminating material produced is epitomized by this answer from a branch children's librarian.

I would be holding an armful of books and the telephone receiver while answering enquiries from at least three children and a teacher, at the same time trying to prevent several small boys from practising kung-fu kicks on each other. The clock would show 5.30, the bookshelves would be in semi-chaos and I would look rather distracted.

Choice of this final example of qualitative technique contains a moral. Sergean was a skilled and experienced industrial psychologist. Perhaps the rest of us, frequently less well qualified to venture into the exposed no-man's land of qualitative research, should seek help more often from such experts. At the very least, we should try adapting tests they have used to our purposes, before embarking on the dangerous course of designing new tests of our own devising.

Reading list and references
1 Antaki, C., *Analysing everyday explanation: a casebook of methods*, London, Sage, 1988.
2 Banaka, W. H., *Training in depth-interviewing*, London, Harper & Row, 1972.
3 Bogdan, R., and Taylor, S. J., *Introduction to qualitative research methods*, New York, Wiley, 1984.
4 Budd, M., 'The readers' advisory situation in the public library: the significance of non-verbal communication', *Journal of librarianship*, **9**, (1), 1977, 29–37.
5 Cronin, B., *The education of library/information professionals: a conflict of objectives*, London, Aslib, 1982 (Occasional publication 28).
6 Douglas, J. D., *Creative interviewing*, London, Sage, 1985.
7 Fenton, R., 'Nonverbal communication between librarians and patrons', *New Zealand libraries*, **43**, (5), 1981, 85–7.
8 Forbes, R., and Jackson, P., 'Non-verbal behaviour', *Journal of occupational psychology*, **53**, (1), 1980, 65.
9 Goode, W. J., and Hatt, P. K., *Methods in social research*, Tokyo, London, McGraw-Hill Kogakusha, 1952.
10 Goodyear, M., 'Qualitative research: is this the industrial revolution or are we re-inventing the wheel?', *Market Research Society newsletter*, 254, May 1987, 26–7.
11 Greenblat, C. S., *Designing games and simulations*, London, Sage, 1988.
12 Griggs, S., 'Analysing qualitative data', *Journal of the Market Research Society*, **29**, (1), 1987, 15–34.
13 Groves, R., and Kahn, R. L., *Surveys by telephone: a national comparison with personal interviews*, London, Academic Press, 1980.

14 Henerson, M. E., *et al.*, *How to measure attitudes*, London, Sage, 1988.
15 Hoinville, G., and Jowell, R., *Survey research practice*, London, Heinemann, 1982.
16 Hughes, J. A., *Sociological analysis: methods of discovery*, London, Nelson, 1976.
17 Kahn, R. L., and Cannell, C. F., *The dynamics of interviewing: theory, techniques and cases*, New York, Wiley, 1983.
18 Kazlauskas, E., 'An exploratory study: a kinesic analysis of academic public library service points', *Journal of academic librarianship*, **2**, (3), 1976, 130–4.
19 McCracken, G., *The long interview*, London, Sage, 1988.
20 McDonald, C., *Telephone surveys: a review of research findings*, London, Market Research Society Development Fund, 1981.
21 Mahoney, M. J., *Scientist as subject: the psychological imperative*, Cambridge, Mass., Ballinger, 1976.
22 Moore, N., *The emerging market for librarians and information workers*, London, British Library, 1987 (LIR report 56).
23 Moore, N., *How to do research*, London, Library Association, 1987.
24 Morris, D., *Manwatching: a field guide to human behaviour*, London, Cape, 1977, London, Panther, 1978 (paperback).
25 Oppenheim, A. N., *Questionnaire design and attitude measurement*, Aldershot, Gower, 1968.
26 Patton, M. Q., *Creative evaluation*, London, Sage, 1987.
27 Patton, M. Q., *How to use qualitative methods in evaluation*, London, Sage, 1988.
28 Pease, K., *Communication with and without words*, New York, Vernon Scott, 1974.
29 Reason, P., *Human enquiry in action: developments in new paradigm research*, London, Sage, 1988.
30 Ritchie, J., 'The contribution of qualitative methods to social policy', *Survey methods newsletter*, Winter 1985/6, 9–10.
31 Sergean, R., McKay, J. R., and Corkill, C. M., *The Sheffield Manpower Project: a survey of staffing requirements for librarianship and information work*, Sheffield University, Postgraduate School of Librarianship and Information Science, 1976.
32 Slater, M., *Career patterns and the occupational image: a study of the library/information field*, London, Aslib, 1980 (Occasional publication 23).
33 Slater, M., 'Manpower forecasting and planning', *Journal of information science*, **1**, (3), 1979, 131–43.
34 Slater, M., *Non-use of library-information resources at the workplace: a comparative study of users and non-users of onsite industrial-commercial services*, London, Aslib, 1984 (Research report 7).
35 Turner, C. F., and Martin, E., *Surveying subjective phenomena*, New York, Sage, 1985, 2 vols.
36 Wynn, H., 'Observation versus controlled experimentation', *Survey methods newsletter*, Spring/Summer 1986, 5–6.
37 Yin, R. K., *Case study research: design and methods*, London, Sage, 1985.

8 Analysing qualitative material

Helen Finch

Fieldwork is near complete; notes assembled; tape-recordings piling up. What now?

Analysis will, in fact, already have started. It is not just 'the next stage'. But little literature exists on how to go about it. Researchers new to qualitative methods can feel lost in the sheer mass of detail they encounter.

This chapter looks at the processes involved in working with qualitative data to discover a meaning and understanding in relation to a research objective. It considers first the role or purpose of analysis in this context, and some general principles involved in carrying it out. It then describes, in a fairly mechanistic way, a method of analysis.

This is not upheld as the sole way to proceed. Individual researchers will have their own modus operandi. Strategies will need to take account, too, of the type of data being handled, the focus of the research objective, and the use and users of the results. But an example of a particular approach is outlined (along with its context) in order to illustrate one way that the issues pertinent to any analysis, may be applied in practice. Theoretical discussion alone can be too generalized or esoteric as a background for suggesting a course of action. Qualitative analysis is not magic. Much of it is painstaking and laborious – necessarily so, if the central issue of validity is to be addressed.

For this reason the emphasis of the chapter is more on an empirical approach. It draws on experience, as a professional researcher, working mostly in the domain of applied social policy research: investigating specific issues within the fields of health, housing, education, employment, transport, or other aspects of social/cultural life. Whatever the research question, the broad orientation of the studies has been the same: an attempt to step into the shoes of the participants in the research to view the issue, without preconception, from their point of view. Methods of analysis, though tailored to an extent for each project, have also been broadly similar across the studies.

This sets something of a frame of reference, which will become more explicit later in the chapter. Qualitative research covers a range of methods and research practices. It is hoped that the strategies described here, combined with the discussion on central issues in analysis, might trigger ideas in the reader for adapting methods to suit particular projects and serve as a springboard for an individual plan of action.

1. The role of analysis and the general processes involved

1.1 *Starting point*
Certain key elements are central to the role or purpose of analysis in qualitative research. Analysis entails:

a quest for valid meaning or understanding,

from the data,

in relation to a research objective.

The same could be said of survey data analysis. But due to the differences of qualitative design (in both its methods and its aims) these principles take on a different slant. As a starting point in considering the analysis of qualitative material, each one of the above elements is therefore briefly considered. This is used as a framework for discussion of other related issues concerning the process of analysis and what it involves.

1.2 *Objectives, data, and valid interpretation*
First, the research objective, the question (or questions) addressed by the research, will be a basis of any strategy for analysis of qualitative data. Qualitative studies can have widely differing aims. These might be broad or focused, academic or applied. They may be achieved by description alone, though are also likely to call for interpretation, and perhaps evaluation. It is possible that recommendations may be required. They might be used to inform a policy decision or a marketing decision, or to test a theory. But the analytic strategies used in any of these differing cases will be responsive to the research objective, just as the study design, and the manner in which answers to the questions are sought in the field, will relate to it. This is not to say that serendipitous findings are not possible, nor that the analysis may not go up some blind alleys. Other questions may perhaps be answered by the analysis along the way, and other uses for the data become apparent. The research objective however will be a central thread running through the analytic strategy.

Despite this diversity, qualitative studies share the same broad type of aim, which contrasts with that of quantitative surveys. The qualitative approach is concerned with understanding the nature of a part of the social world, as far as possible from the perspective and context of the actors within it. It does not attempt to describe issues in the social world through measurement. Differences between the two approaches are described in detail elsewhere in this book. An important implication for qualitative analysis however is that its differing type of objective sets a different meaning to the concept of validity, as will be discussed below.

Secondly, the analysis will be based on the data. This may seem too obvious a point to state. But it is not just description that is required from the data. Conceptual frameworks, that may be used as tools in the analysis, will also need to be derived as far as possible from within the data; and interpretation and theorizing will similarly need to be *grounded* in it – to use Glaser and Strauss's (1967) term. Several further issues arise out of the nature of qualitative data, and the role of the researcher in analysing it.

The data comes from listening to, and observing, the people taking part in the study. It consists of: words – attitudes, accounts, explanations – as expressed by the participants, in their own style of language and personal meaning; and observations and impressions from the researcher; all set against a background framework of the researcher's existing knowledge and experience. When analysing qualitative data, the researcher plays a dual role. Partly, he or she works as a technician, systematically performing 'objective' and definable tasks. Yet also, by virtue of being human, and a participant in the study as researcher-interviewer-observer, the researcher is an instrument of the analysis. The researcher brings things to bear upon the data. Against the backcloth of his or her cultural knowledge, including perhaps personal experience of the subject under study, and predispositions regarding it, will be reactions to the findings: surprises perhaps, and intuitive thoughts or ideas triggered by it. These too will be used in the analysis.

The need to validate the way in which this is done, avoiding researcher bias, clearly becomes paramount. Before considering the central issues of validity however, it is worth noting some further implications (which relate also to it) arising from the premise that the analysis comes from the data. For example, the importance of knowing the contents of the data becomes evident: the basic requirement, in conducting an analysis, for the researcher to become thoroughly familiar with the range and detail of the issues contained in it. This can only be built up by handling all the data in a systematic way. And knowledge of the data must not be in too fragmented a form. Awareness of the relationships within the data, and of the dynamics between different sections of it, needs to be retained, and processes observed in their totality. Knowledge is needed of the issues both within each individual interview/case and between all interviews/cases. Throughout the analysis there is also a need for clarity in how interpretations are derived; and, importantly, a need to be conscious of the limitations and boundaries of the data, of what questions it cannot, validly, answer.

The quest for valid meaning or understanding, seeking that the emergent picture from the analysis is a true picture of what is being studied, needs to be addressed constantly throughout the analysis, as it does at all stages of the study – from design, through data gathering, and presentation. The different types of 'emergent picture' sought in qualitative research, from that required in quantitative research, is the reference point which determines the meaning of validity in this context. It will seek to identify issues, and the ways that the issues interrelate, as a means of explaining and understanding the situation under study. It cannot validly address extent – for example the extent that an attitude, or a pattern of behaviour, occurs – although key issues will be distinguishable from peripheral issues, as relating to the subject of study.

Within this boundary, a valid picture can still only be built up if the validity issue is addressed on a procedural level all the way through the analysis. Some ways of doing this have already been outlined above, and will be further specified throughout the account which follows. They relate mainly to the need for the analysis to be entrenched in the data at all stages, and systematically and rigorously built up in it – all the time questioning the nature of the evidence and its boundaries, being aware of its limitations. They also arise from the need for the researcher to make conscious, and to monitor his or her involvement in the analysis, including initial predispositions regarding the subject, interaction with the respondent in the interview, and the basis on which intuitive guesses or feelings about the data may be confirmed (or contradicted) from the evidence. Methods of cross-checking conclusions and interpretations from the data need also to be incorporated, for example in consultation with co-researchers, with others who may use the research and, where possible, returning to the respondents of the research for their reactions. A final requirement as a validity check is that both procedures and evidence from the analysis are clear and accessible to others to authenticate the conclusions reached.

1.3 *The process of analysis*

Analysis is a process of discovery, reflection and review. It is similar say to chemical analysis of a substance in that it requires first a 'dissolving' or 'loosening' of the constituent parts for examination. The themes and issues of the qualitative data thus exposed are then considered: patterns are sought, contradictions examined, unexpected findings reviewed. This is followed by a 'distilling' of that learned knowledge – a search for essential features, which may be a synthesis of many of the parts, and a rejection of others (in relation to the research objective). Knowledge of the data thus becomes refined. The emergent story is identified and described. With further review (and often precipitated by the process of describing that story) meanings beyond the literal become apparent, implications seen, and the analysis moves beyond description to interpretation and theorizing. Verification, anchoring the abstract back in the data or checking out other evidence, continues the process: the story becomes refined further, the focus sharpened.

All this is a time-consuming and thoughtful process. It requires certain key activities on the part of the researcher, including:

- familiarization – building up knowledge of themes and issues contained in the data;
- systematic description of the contents of the data in an accessible and reduced form, probably grouped within themes;
- reflection on that description, looking at patterns, causal links, repetition and divergence;
- explanation of what appears, from the data, to be going on and not just in a literal sense but in a more abstract or generalized way, with implications of meaning considered;
- interpretation in relation to the research objective;
- checking out that interpretation as far as possible;
- description and discussion of the emergent story (of the interpretation and the evidence for it).

2. Steps toward an analysis

This section takes a more mechanistic approach. Having set out certain general principles and processes involved in the analysis of qualitative data, the intention is now to describe a way of carrying it out.

This however is no simple task. A full portrayal of the analysis process would involve discussion of all the stages of a qualitative research project, from its outset, not just after data collection is complete. It is hard too to describe certain of the activities involved (for example, how to conceptualize from data). And some of the activities overlap: description of a sequence of steps is itself artificial for an organic process in which not all procedures progress sequentially but move rather more in spirals than straight lines.

The account is in three stages. First, some background parameters are set out, defining the general research practice on which it is based. This is followed by a summary of some initial steps toward an analysis that may take place from the outset of the study, as fieldwork progresses. Having set the scene, the final section then outlines strategies for analysing qualitative data in its entirety, once data collection is complete.

2.1 *Assumptions behind this account*
To summarize: the account that follows refers to the type of qualitative research that investigates a specific objective by means of lengthy unstructured interviews which are tape-recorded and usually transcribed. The research objective is likely to require a description or explanation of the situation under study (through understanding of the perspective of the participants in the research). Accompanying suggestions or ideas, or an evaluation of the situation, may also be needed. The researcher who undertakes the analysis is involved in all stages of the study.

2.1.1 *In-depth interviews*
The focus of the account is on the analysis of material from in-depth interviews with individuals. Some additional points are made about the handling of group discussion data. But material obtained through other qualitative methods – participant observation, the use of video, or the analysis of documentary evidence, for example – is not specifically included.

The interviews are unstructured in the sense that although certain themes or topics central to the purpose of the research are covered in each, the way that those topics are approached (including perhaps the order in which they come up, the extent of discussion within each, and the range of issues discussed), will vary. This variation is shaped largely by the person being interviewed. The aim in conducting the interview is to enable the person to express their point of view fully and in their own way with minimal influence from the researcher.

A 'topic guide', itemizing main issues to be covered in relation to the research objective, is used by the researcher when conducting the interviews. This will be drawn up at the start of the study when mapping out the territory to be explored. It is based on the researcher's perception so far of the central issues of the study – informed by consultation of any existing literature relating to its subject matter, and discussions with experts or others able to provide a background perspective.

The topic guide is not only an *aide memoire* of essential points of enquiry. It also provides an initial framework for the researcher's thoughts on the subject of study: around which data and observations are built up in the field. As such it is, in a sense, the starting point of the analysis: a loose framework that may become overturned and certainly will be fleshed out, added to, given emphasis, as the fieldwork progresses.

2.1.2 *Few interviews, though rich in data*

The numbers of people interviewed, and therefore of cases for analysis, will be far fewer than any sample size required for a structured survey. The rigorous techniques needed in the analysis could not, in practical terms, be applied to large numbers. Nor are large numbers necessary. Since the aim is to understand an issue in depth rather than to measure its incidence, there comes a point beyond which additional cases offer diminishing return. My own experience has been on studies involving on average about 20 to 40 interviews (sometimes supplemented with group discussions), and interviews have typically lasted about one-and-a-half hours in length. These figures are quoted only as context to the account that follows. Numbers, and duration, of interviews should be as long as they need to be, given the objective, and will vary for different studies.

The term 'sample' would be inappropriate in this context. The people taking part have been purposely selected: they may share a common characteristic which is at the basis of the investigation, whilst representing a range in terms of other characteristics (socio-demographic or other variables). Or there may be two or three distinct sub-groups chosen for differing perspectives (for example, users and non-users of a service). During the analysis decisions will be made on which variable would be the clearest basis for ordering charts of the data, though this is impossible to discern at the outset.

The interview data will be detailed and lengthy. Accounts of attitudes, experiences, behaviour, histories, and expectations, may all be contained in it. The context in which these arise will also be apparent, and will constitute additional material to add to the picture. This applies both to circumstances described by respondents as context to their situation or point of view, and to the way that issues arise in the interview. Emotions, points of emphasis or indifference, of awareness or ignorance, may also be demonstrated. There may too be contradictions in the data within an interview.

2.1.3 *Tape-recordings and verbatim transcripts*
The nature of the data, and the method of achieving it (requiring the interviewer to be fully alert and quietly responsive during the interview) make it imperative, for most studies, that the interviews are tape-recorded. Note-taking is rarely an adequate substitute: distracting both interviewer and interviewee, and leading to selective reporting. All the detail and language is required.

Transcriptions are produced from the recordings. As verbatim accounts, more accessible than taped data, and able to be marked up and annotated, they constitute the main material for the analysis and are central to the method described here. (This account does not extend to the use of computer-assisted techniques in analysing material transcribed directly onto word processor or computer. See Pfaffenberger (1988), for example, or McCracken (1988), for discussion of the use of computer technology in this context.)

Analysis from a transcript may need to be supplemented by listening additionally to the tape-recording of the interview. Passages of transcript may be indistinct or obviously inaccurate for instance, or there may be sections where it is useful to listen to intonation. For interviews conducted by a co-researcher, or by someone other than the person undertaking the analysis, the tape-recording provides a far more vivid feel of the situation of the interview. However, transcripts of interviews conducted personally are generally sufficient for bringing to mind feelings and observations about the interview without the need to listen to the tape (unless there has been a lengthy time-lapse between interviewing and analysis).

The arduous task of producing verbatim transcripts is best left to an agency specializing in this service. Attempts to transcribe a set of tapes any other way are fraught by the sheer tedium of the mechanics of the task. There are better ways of using that time more effectively on the analysis.

2.1.4 *Researcher-interviewer-analyst*

The researcher who undertakes the analysis also carries out a substantial number of the interviews. The analysis of interview material collected by others is, I find, far harder and more time consuming to analyse fully. In such cases, extensive notes and/or discussions with the interviewer are required as backup. To have, instead, a visual image and memory of the actual experience of an interview, even of apparently irrelevant details of it, renders all of that interview data more readily accessible at the later stages of the analysis.

2.2 *Initial steps – in the field*

The reader will by now have an idea of the extent, nature and format of the main data needing analysis. Before describing ways of working systematically with that data, some preliminary steps toward analysis, that may take place throughout the data collection stage of the project, are described here. Mainly these are ways of obtaining further information – grist to the mill, to add to the analysis. They also cover ways of checking out as you go along, and the beginnings of organizing for the main analysis by making the data more readily accessible at later stages.

2.2.1 *Recruitment observations*

Participants in a qualitative study can be recruited in different ways. Whether the cooperation of named individuals is sought (each known to fulfil a certain sample requirement), or whether specified quotas of respondent-types need finding, initial reactions to the study, and response rates in terms of agreement/disagreement to take part, can provide additional data. It is useful to note recruitment experiences. Relative reluctance (or eagerness) to participate in the study, perhaps on the part of certain types of people and not others, might tie in with attitudes expressed in the interviews, or suggest further areas of questioning in relation to the subject of study.

2.2.2 *Interviewing technique: obtaining, reviewing and using data in the field*

Some points about interviewing technique and how they relate to the shifting frame of reference for the analysis are described here since it is obviously crucial that valid data for analysis is obtained.

Much thought and discussion will have gone into the research design and the compiling of the topic guide (as described above) – which in a sense sets an initial frame of reference for the analysis. Thoughts and hypotheses from that stage however get pushed aside at the start of the interview. The interviewer needs to approach first with an open mind. Awareness of the research objective is sufficient, and perhaps some basic background information about the type of respondent, at that stage. The topic guide will be used only as backup and as a reminder of essential topics for coverage.

There will be a shape to the interview: different phases reached through changes in gear. Setting the scene in the introduction, the research topic and some background to it is outlined in general terms, recalling the information provided when the person was recruited to take part, and providing further assurances of confidentiality. The opening of the interview then starts with fairly neutral or general questions, so that the person starts to relax and talk, but avoids if possible too much depth on key issues too soon. This builds up to detailed exploration of those issues later in the interview. The various topics for coverage may evolve from each other as the respondent talks, or the interviewer may need to take more active measures to introduce them. Time will also need to be allowed for the person to unwind at the end. Due to these different phases of the interview, there will be surplus data generated that will need to be sifted through in the main stage of the analysis.

The basic tactics or skills required of the interviewer include: the asking of simple open-ended questions, avoidance of prompting or leading questions, but extensive use of probing ('tell me more about that' etc.), never assuming meaning but seeking elaboration. The interviewer should allow silences to occur, and will adopt as far as possible an attentive listening role, encouraging or reassuring as necessary. Mental notes will be made of what is being left unsaid (in relation here to the topic guide) as well as noting the language and substance of points raised. This information can be used later in the interview – to formulate further questions or to play back to the person to seek their reactions.

The topic guide is likely to be amended after the initial few interviews. Unforeseen items may have arisen for example, that need exploring in subsequent interviews. And there is nothing wrong in making use of interview data or observations (or thoughts arising from them) in subsequent interviews. In this way hypotheses for the analysis can develop or progress as the fieldwork proceeds.

2.2.3 *Notes after each interview*

Supplementary information about an interview, recorded by the interviewer on its completion, can both provide additional material of direct relevance to the study, and contribute to the process of analysis. Partly, these initial notes will be external observations: of the person's manner and approach perhaps, of what was said when the tape-recorder was turned off, or other contextual details surrounding the interviewing situation that might be relevant to its subject matter. Partly also these notes can be internal impressions and thoughts – feelings about how the interview went, or immediate reactions to aspects of the data that have come up. Fresh hypotheses or ideas may come to mind which can be put to the test or looked out for in subsequent interviews, as described above.

If not recorded as fieldwork progresses, these observations and impressions tend to get forgotten or jumbled between cases. They can however be hurriedly spoken onto the tape in private at the end of the interview (and later transcribed along with it), or written in note form.

This brief initial consideration and review while still close to the interview is a first – raw – stage of the analysis, likely to be modified at later stages, but nevertheless valuable in building up the picture. A brief time spent in this way at this stage makes for easier recall later: somehow it is more likely to fix the whole interview in mind. And it is especially necessary for any interviews that are conducted by someone other than the researcher who will carry out the analysis.

2.2.4 *Discussion with colleagues*

Comparison of these impressions and experiences with those of any co-researchers working on the project is valuable particularly in the early stages of fieldwork. How do their views and experiences of interviews compare with yours? What are their observations, surprises, problems? What sort of material have they found is coming out so far? Is the topic guide working? (Why not? Might it need amending?) This kind of discussion both acts as a kind of validity check on your own ideas, and generates more.

2.2.5 *Indexing interviews: an overview as the fieldwork progresses*

One of the problems in analysing qualitative data is that there is so much of it. Any action that may render it more manageable or accessible is useful. For example, as fieldwork progresses, a simple index of the interviews can be compiled, summarizing certain descriptive characteristics of each one. This provides an overview of the interviews carried out. It can be useful as a check on the balance of the sample in relation to the original design, and in relation to any additional factors that may be emerging as pertinent (and may therefore warrant further investigation with more interviews of that type). It is also useful, at a later stage, as an index to the transcripts, and as a framework to which further descriptive variables or comments may be added.

It is a good idea to do this on sheets of A3 paper, with respondents identified by serial numbers down the side of the page and the characteristics itemized across the page – with plenty of space remaining on which later observations may be added. The descriptive variables itemized might show the gender, age, class, household situation, or other characteristics pertinent to the subject of study – housing characteristics perhaps, services used, etc. The cases might be listed in the order in which they are interviewed, or they may be grouped by a central variable – area, site, or another key characteristic.

For group discussions, a list or diagrammatic seating plan of participants in each group can be drawn up showing the same type of individual characteristics.

2.2.6 *Recording the interview*
Any steps that will enhance the quality of the interview recording, and thence the accuracy of the transcript, are basic preliminaries too for the analysis. Such steps include: recording in stereo; onto 90-minute tapes (longer tapes are apt to break or tangle); frequent cleaning and de-magnetizing of the recording head of the machine; and reduction of background noise as far as possible during the interview.

I make no excuse for mentioning these basic practicalities as a preliminary to an account of steps in an analysis. The tapes, and from them the transcripts, are the key materials on which that analysis will be based. Although attention to the recording equipment and conditions of the interview will still not necessarily lead to transcripts of perfect accuracy, errors are reduced, and the time-consuming process of having to listen to the tape is less likely to be needed.

2.3 **The main stage: analysis of the data in its entirety when fieldwork is complete**
With data collection complete, the main stage of analysis starts. Miles and Huberman (1984) describe three 'concurrent flows of activity' involved in it: data reduction, data display and

conclusion drawing/verification (all of which they explore in depth, with examples, in their book). The following description illustrates one way of putting these into practice. Other accounts by qualitative researchers of individual methods of analysis are described by Davies and Esseveld (1987), and Jones (1985).

The method described here entails the following stages:
- initial familiarization with issues arising
- compiling a list of key themes
- systematically indexing all the data
- charting the data's themes
- refining the charted material
- describing the emergent story.

2.3.1 *Step one: Initial familiarization with issues arising*
The first step is one of standing back and taking an initial look at the contents of the data. It involves reading through some (perhaps all) of the transcripts and field notes, becoming familiar with their contents, and discerning and noting the various issues that arise in them. (Tape-recordings might be used at this stage as an alternative, or additional, to the transcripts.)

First impressions of what in broad terms is represented in the data, are mulled over, as well as any thoughts or reactions to it, or hypotheses for later investigation. Ideas on ways that the data might appropriately be grouped are also noted, as well as differences between types of interviews (the index described above in 2.2.5 of the previous section is useful here, and can be further added to).

The questions in the researcher's mind when reading the transcripts are mainly along the lines of: 'What is this person saying? What issues is he/she raising? What broader or more general concerns are those issues part of?' The research objective will also be a broad point of reference. But thoughts or influences that went into the compiling of the topic guide will at present be put aside. The researcher needs to approach now with an open mind and a fresh spirit of discovery: to look at the detailed content of the data, and to start to think about what, in broader terms, is represented there.

If not all of the transcripts are consulted at this initial stage, a variety of different types of interview need to be included. The nature of the cross-section will depend on the objective of the study and the variables covered in its design. Certain socio-demographic characteristics may need to be taken into account for example, or behavioural types. Additional variables may have emerged as particularly relevant to the subject under study and a variety of interviews that characterize these will also need to be included. The index described above is useful at this stage, presenting an overview of the many variables, and therefore suggesting transcripts for study.

2.3.2 *Step two: Compiling a list of key themes*

So far, the list of issues found within the data will be multifarious and uneven, containing observations and items of varying levels of generalization or specificity. Some of the items listed may for example be aspects or sub-divisions of a broader issue. Some may be applicable to just one type of respondent. The next step is to refine the list into a collection of key themes that summarize in broad terms the issues that appear to be in the data: moving further away from the detail of what is being said, towards a general identification and definition of the themes representing that detail.

This involves a grouping of the issues, under a number of central themes or topics. Following on the process of the previous stage, the researcher continues to question: 'What broader or more general concerns might these issues be grouped under?', and continues to remember the research objective. The sub-issues that relate to themes can also be grouped under them, and perhaps ordered.

The topic guide used when conducting the interviews also outlined themes and issues. The list that emerges now may show a similarity to the topic guide, but it will also contain important differences. It arises from the data: there will be additional points and perspectives that alter original issues.

The list will be used in later stages of the analysis. A systematic and rigorous examination of all the data will be undertaken within its broad framework. That is not to say that the framework is fixed rigid — it will still be open to subsequent modification as understanding of the data increases during the process of carrying out the analysis. New themes may be added or the framework slightly altered.

Two examples are given below (to which reference is made again when considering later steps of the analysis):

Example one: In a study examining factors influencing dental attendance, where the key objective was to understand barriers to attendance ('Why do many people in need of dental treatment not take it up?'), the key broad groupings were as follows: behaviour and beliefs regarding dental health and general health (including parents' and children's behaviour/beliefs as reported by the respondent); views on various component aspects of a dental visit; and on dentists (approach, manner, a 'good dentist', dentists compared with doctors, etc.); perceived barriers to dental attendance (under the broad headings of cost, fear, past experiences, perception of need, and 'main' barrier); ideas/suggestions for breaking down the barriers. Within all but the last of these themes a number of subdivisions or related issues were specified.

Example two: In a small-scale study examining how academic researchers conducted their research (with the objective of seeing if, and how, the research process was affected by cuts in library expenditure), nine key themes were used to analyse the data. The broad groupings were: general site-specific issues; general book issues; periodical issues; photocopying; use of other libraries; by-passing libraries; library services effects; longer term effects on research/cutting corners in research; effects on students/teaching.

2.3.3 *Step three: Systematically indexing the data*
The type of list described above now becomes an index that is applied to all the data. Similar to the way that, in structured surveys, answers to open-ended questions are coded from a *code-frame*, so codes for each theme in the qualitative data are marked where they occur.

In practical terms this means reading through each transcript (and accompanying notes) annotating sections of data with the relevant theme codes. Codes might be in the form of numbers, letters, key words, or a combination of these: for example, 2c, to indicate a subsection of a particular theme, or 2 to indicate a general point on that theme which is not coded further.

Some pages or sections of data will have several codes marked on them (where themes overlap), as well as remarks, thoughts, questions, highlighting – added by the researcher when working through them. Other pages will remain unannotated. They may for example contain contextual material about the respondent that is already noted in the index or elsewhere. Or they may contain material that, although essential to the dynamic of the interview and the way in which it took place, is not actually relevant to the research objective.

This may sound a fairly structured approach for dealing with qualitative data: rather like segmenting it into boxes. But the themes or categories are not rigidly fixed: they are likely to be expanded and developed further throughout this stage (and beyond) as understanding of the data builds up. Meanwhile the data remains in the context in which it arose.

This step in the analysis is therefore one of getting to know the data further, and in a systematic way. It is also the start of rendering more accessible the themes and issues contained in it – that will be continued as the data becomes further reduced in the next stage.

2.3.4 *Step four: Charting the data's themes*

The next step is one of displaying the data, in distilled form, in such a way that all the data relating to a particular theme or issue can be viewed together (across all interviews), whilst retaining a sense of its relationship to other themes (within individual interviews). It is important that the internal totality of any one interview is preserved as far as possible. The context and relationships between themes in any one case need to be considered as much as the overview between cases.

A method of doing this is by summarizing on two-way charts. Working through a marked-up transcript, the researcher extracts and outlines sections of the data in columns designated for the different themes and their sub-sections. Large sheets of paper (e.g. A3) might be used for this purpose: with the themes as column headings across the top of the page so that the various sections of the interview are described in the appropriate column. A line is ruled across to mark the boundary between that interview's data and the next. Subsequent cases are plotted beneath this, also extending across the columns. The end result is that the data may be viewed two ways: across, for the picture of an individual interview, and down, for cumulative data on a theme (arising in different interviews).

A number of practicalities in the charting method need consideration – both in addressing the issue of validity, and with forethought to the next steps in the analysis. Considering first the structure of the charts: thought needs to be given to the most appropriate grouping and ordering of the columns for example, and even to the approximate width of columns relative to each other. The number of different types of charts necessary to cover the data will depend on the nature of the study and its breadth. There may be one chart for each broad theme or section of the data, each containing different columns for sub-categories of it. This was the case in Example one (the dental study) above: five different chart formats were used, corresponding to the five groupings described, with columns for related issues within each grouping. In Example two (on academic research procedures and library cuts) the focus was more specific; there were just two different chart formats: covering, respectively, the first five and the last three themes described. In order to cover data from all the interviews carried out, I find it is generally necessary for about two or three versions of any one chart to be completed (though this will depend of course on the number of interviews, and types of issues charted).

The order of the columns in any chart may suggest itself from the data, and in relation to the research objective. For some studies the order that the themes are emergent in most of the interviews may be appropriate – these might relate for example to a sequence in time, or a flow of events. Alternatively, a logical order may be apparent from other ways that the themes link to each other. Columns for related topics may be best next to each other, or it may be useful on occasion to view adjacent contrasting topics for direct comparison.

The grouping of the individual interviews/cases on the charts also needs consideration. There may be a key characteristic within which it would be useful to group the charted data from the interviews. This might be by age grouping, social class, gender, site/location of the interview, etc. – it depends on the research objective, and on impressions so far of differences within the data and what is the main determinant of those differences. In the dental study, interview data was grouped on the charts within three bands corresponding to frequency of dental attendance: regular, irregular, and non-attenders.

When transferred from the transcripts to the charts, the reduced data is likely at this stage to be mainly descriptive: a summary representation of relevant data from each transcript. The flavour of each interview is retained as far as possible, in language and phrasing, in an attempt to remain close to the data albeit in this summary form. And there needs to be a clear demarcation of what is the language (or direct quotation) from the respondent as distinct from material that is summarized from the interview by the researcher-analyst. Similarly, any interpretation of the data, which may be recorded on the charts at this stage, needs to be clearly indicated as such.

This step of systematically compiling charts brings increased familiarity with all the contents of the data, as well as simpler access to it for the later stage of the analysis. The beginnings of interpretation or abstraction from the data (described more in the next step below) may also start as the charting progresses. Thoughts that occur to the researcher when working with a particular transcript in this way, or a synthesis of certain elements in a transcript, may be noted down on the chart. Assessments or judgements of an individual interview/case (or of aspects of it), relevant to the research objective, might also be made at this stage. These can be recorded systematically onto the chart, adopting a new column for that purpose, or can be added to an existing column, or to the index. In the dental study for example, a summary assessment was made for each irregular-/non-attender of what in their particular case appeared to be the main barrier to dental attendance. This needed to be done at this stage, close to all the data for that interview.

The completed charts therefore contain mainly description (in summarized form, with some quotations or references to relevant page numbers of the transcript), and the beginnings of some interpretation and assessment of the data, though this latter activity is mainly postponed until the next stage.

2.3.5 *Step five: Refining the charted material*
By now the data is in a distilled and more accessible form and the researcher has an extensive awareness of what is there. The next step is one of again standing back: reflecting on the data in its new condensed format, and considering alongside it any other material (e.g. fieldnotes, impressions recalled from the interviews, recruitment observations, index, backup statistical data, etc.). First thoughts on the subject are also remembered (from the pre-fieldwork stage, when the design and topic guide were considered) and are compared with what has been found.

This step constitutes a more direct quest for meaning in relation to the research objective. It is the start of formally putting together the full answer to the research question. A meaningful synthesis needs now to be derived from the data – which necessitates moving further away from its detail to a more generalized or abstract level.

This is carried out by reflective examination of the charts and other material described above. Discussion with co-researchers involved on the project is also very helpful at this stage.

Strategies include: searching for patterns or links between sections of data; grouping of similar or related themes that have emerged (which may be different from groupings adopted so far); distinguishing emphasis – between key and peripheral issues, or between groups of respondents; counting frequency – of mention of an issue or of an attitude, etc.; looking at differences between subgroups (and identifying the cause of the differences); and examining unexpected data, or findings that are apparently contradictory, attempting to isolate the cause of this. Variables that were thought to be salient in earlier stages of the analysis (for example in structuring the charts) are likely now to be refined. New issues of greater salience, which may or may not relate to those determined earlier, will now come into focus.

A small number of further summary charts may be compiled, based on the synthesized material. These can provide a sharper overview of the issues in the data that relate to a more general or abstract issue within it. They are built up of evidence from the original charts. The original charts will be annotated, and comparative rating systems may be applied to sections of charted material. Typologies or flow diagrams may be built up.

Overall, this step involves questioning the data, looking for relationships between variables, and testing out ideas or hypotheses. As an instrument of the analysis, the researcher notes his/her own reactions to what is found — whether these be guesses as to meaning, instinctive reactions, surprises — and consciously uses these to question further and develop ideas. The researcher then goes back to the data (either to the charts, transcripts, or tapes) for verification. This backwards and forwards process will be repeated from here on in the analysis to ensure that the explanation or interpretation is grounded.

2.3.6 *Step six: Describing the emergent story*
Analysis continues in the description and communication of the emergent story from the research. The discipline of thinking through a logical and coherent format when preparing to present to others what has been found, in itself tends to trigger more ideas and clarify understanding. These can be confirmed or added to in discussion. Further questions can be raised for checking back in the data. Other people's reactions to the data can be taken into account. And the evidence and analytic strategy, as well as the interpretation, will need to be revealed: the presentation can also serve as a check on researcher bias.

The interpretation from the analysis might be presented and discussed with different types of audiences, including those who may have commissioned the research or who will use the results of it. This is especially necessary in the type of research that investigates issues in order to evaluate or seek answers (rather than purely descriptive research), and particularly if recommendations are called for. Presentation back to the respondents who took part in the research may also be able to be carried out — an excellent means of confirming and sharpening the findings.

Oral presentation and discussion needs to be carried out before written reporting. As a further, interactive, stage of analysis, it helps determine the appropriate structure and content of any written report. The necessary balance between description and interpretation can better be judged.

References and further reading

Davies, K., and Esseveld, J., *Reflections on research practices in qualitative research*, Lund University, 1987.

Glaser, B. G., and Strauss, A. L., *The discovery of grounded theory: strategies for qualitative research*, Aldine, New York, 1967.

Jones, S., 'The analysis of depth interviews', *Applied qualitative research*, Walker, R., (ed.), Gower, 1985.

McCracken, G., 'The long interview', *Qualitative research methods*, Volume 13, Sage, 1988.

Miles, M. B., and Huberman, A. M., *Qualitative data analysis. A sourcebook of methods*, Sage, 1984.

Pfaffenberger, B., 'Microcomputer applications in qualitative research', *Qualitative research methods*, Volume 14, Sage, 1988.

Ritchie, J., and Sykes, W., (eds.), *Advanced workshop in applied qualitative research*, SCPR, 1986.

9 Observation and after

David Streatfield

> I stand and look around, and say 'thus does it appear to me and thus
> I seem to see'.
>   William Howard Russell
>   (Victorian war correspondent for *The Times*

1. A day in the life of an observer

My 'observation subject' is tall and dark, aged about 50.
Checking off the items which will help me to perform my 'fly on
the wall' role, I wonder about my Al Capone interview suit.
Does it fit in with his general appearance? He is tidy, tending
towards casual, in a corduroy jacket and floral tie, topped by
heavy rimmed glasses – everyone's idea of a social services
deputy director?

At our initial meeting last week the deputy director, I will call
him John, answered questions about his education and
experience. Although he answered questions readily and
seemed interested in our project I was left with an impression of
remoteness. This caused a certain amount of anxiety to be mixed
with my relief at getting stuck into the observation today.

1.2 *Observation begins*

Had I but known it, the day was to have a perfect start. Over the
next few weeks it emerged that when subjects were enmeshed
in group meetings early in the observation period, this helped
them to get used to the new experience and they soon relaxed
under our scrutiny. We met today in John's office on the fourth
floor of a tower block, half of which is the headquarters of the
department. We left almost immediately for the five-minute walk
to city hall.

On the way to this meeting of the corporate management
group John said, 'I normally arrive fifteen minutes late so they
can resolve the minutes. It's better not to this time because I need
to introduce you.' The meeting is in an archetypal local
government committee room, swamped by a huge table and

with seating capacity for about 40. There are 12 people from different departments at this session and I find myself shaking hands with the chairman and trying to sort out who's who at the same time. Permission was obtained last week for me to sit in at this meeting and I soon find myself positioned behind and to one side of my subject so that I can see what he is doing.

The chairman tells the other participants why I am here and moves smoothly into gear with minute clearance. Meanwhile John hands me back a sketch plan of the names and departments of the people at the table. I begin to feel better about the whole business even though the acoustics in the room are lousy.

For the first quarter of an hour nothing occurs to engage John's interest and he begins to sag slowly under the table. Over the week he frequently uses his body as a boredom-barometer by thrusting out his feet in front of him and leaning back in his chair at the start of a meeting and gradually subsiding until his nose is almost level with the table-top. When something of interest crops up he pulls himself upright and almost literally pitches into the fray.

Two successive agenda items are relevant to social services and the deputy director speaks on both. The chairman nods across at me and says 'You *are* impressive this morning, John'. John half-rises, turns from his chair and drawls 'A'm going 'ome'. He sits down again and gets heavily embroiled in a procedural argument but the meeting is soon over. There is no social chat between John and the others after the meeting, but after leaving he has to turn back to collect a forgotten briefcase. By the time we negotiate the last set of swing doors on this walk we have established the obvious way of doing this. At first, the observer, as guest, tends to be ushered through, but soon John takes precedence. With luck he knows where he's going!

Back in his office he takes up his usual place at his desk, with his back to the window, and I sit to one side about four feet from him. His out-tray is parked within my reach so that I can look at his mail as he deals with it. (We sorted out this arrangement last week.) Paperwork quickly gives way to a series of phone calls and the first one-to-one meeting passes off smoothly; the caller knew that I was around and only nodded in response to John's: 'This is my shadow from Sheffield University' by way of introduction.

The first casual caller of the week, the research officer, comes in with a pile of data sheets from a survey which she is running. She leaves them for him to look at and threatens to call back for them on Wednesday. He dumps them on a spare chair, where they sit undisturbed until she retrieves them. Like the previous caller, she knew that I would be around and no introduction is required.

More telephone calls are made and received, and each involves my subject giving me a brief summary, but this doesn't appear to create undue pressure. It's surprising how much of a phone call you can follow by listening to one end of it, even when you can't be sure what it's about until afterwards. Lunch time arrives not a moment too soon; I've got out of the habit of sitting still for any length of time.

1.3 *Inquisition*
A brisk walk to the local pub with the research officer restores my circulation and I'm now taken up with the delicate game of getting my lunch clear in five minutes less than the time taken by my subject. Fortunately he's gone home to lunch; later on I'll learn just how difficult it is to record conversations in a crowded saloon bar, or to guess when the shop talk will veer off into 'less purposeful' areas.

The research officer puts me neatly on the spot by asking a series of questions which I can't answer yet. Do I get bored? What are my feelings about my subject's contacts and is he driving me mad? With hindsight I can report that observation is only boring if your subject spends long periods mulling over a report or thinking and since most social services work is highly fragmented this wasn't much of a problem. As for feelings about people, the fact that we concentrated on information activities meant that the nature of interpersonal relationships didn't loom large, but paradoxically we found we could identify many subtle under-currents. (Most of these were confirmed later when we reported back.) Observation seems to be the ideal way to get hooked on differences in management style, identify the best hated staff around and discover an interesting range of office flirtations.

Occasional attempts were made to manipulate the observers by feeding us a particular view of the department, or exploit us as an audience or shield against unwanted encounters, but these were rare and the researchers had the advantage of being able to compare notes and impressions at the end of each day. I found that I grew to like all my observation subjects over the course of the week but my feeling about the people they contacted usually remained neutral. As long as they came up with some kind of information exchange I was happy.

More extreme feelings emerged much later when I found

myself trying to categorize apparent inanities or interpret my scribbled notes of a tortuous discussion. In one case, I felt an aversion to the work role of one of my subjects building up when I was preparing a narrative report for him on that week. My reaction was to write a 'true' account and then edit it for presentation, but I think my impression of the bureaucratic part of the system working against the service to clients probably came through anyway.

1.4 *A hot debate might be constructive*

I get back to the office before John, sucking peppermints in case he's a Methodist. Much of the room is taken up by his desk and chair, three other chairs, a bookcase and a four-drawer filing cabinet. His bookcase contains an assortment of books, reports and journals. I will spend half an hour before he arrives tomorrow listing them, only to be told that he's clearing the lot out next week!

After another brief paperwork session the big issue of the week arrives in the ample form of the community work adviser. Jack Douglas has come to discuss next Friday's meeting of the city community work policy group which is trying to piece together a strategy for community work involving all interested departments and agencies. This department's community workers have produced their own unofficial report as a reply to the official document and the first part of the session centres on how to present this to the policy group. The adviser reveals that two of the city councillors on the group have already seen the counter-report. John will have to contact both before deciding on his next move.

During this 15-minute exchange I get the impression that Jack is holding back and only volunteering information when specifically asked, possibly because he is in the difficult position of advising on community work without having line management responsibility for any community workers. They are responsible to their area directors.

A little light comedy develops as the adviser produces a memo and passes it to John. He passes it back, making various comments, and back and forth it goes until it has crossed the desk eight times. Neither of them appears to be aware of this little four-minute Odyssey.

Later in the afternoon John phones Jack again (at his fourth attempt) and asks how he can make contact with the department's community workers. A name is suggested and the woman concerned is found to be in the building so a message is left for her. John answers two more phone calls, deals with a few items and comments: 'It's looking like an abnormal week. There's a drop off in current work so I'm catching up on multifarious little things, some of which have been hanging fire for a long time.' (The rest of the week proves to be more typical, with plenty of meetings and some pressure.)

Two more meetings and more phone calls (one involving a homeless immigrant family) occur before Margaret Williams, the community work spokesperson arrives. I'm introduced and she looks suspicious and then puzzled. I'm puzzled too, then remember meeting her at a community action meeting in Manchester a year ago. I say nothing because the moment has passed. They spend a quarter of an hour discussing the counter-report in general and its unfavourable comments about work in other departments in particular. John says that he will have to phone the two councillors, before deciding his next move. He sees the report as useful but spoilt by unnecessary comments on other departments; she believes that a hot debate might well be constructive. Several volumes could be filled with what neither of them is choosing to say at this point. John's tone of voice has become slightly flat but hard.

1.5 *A rabbit before a stoat*
She leaves and two minor indicators of fatigue begin to make themselves apparent. I'm getting cramp in my writing hand (the only time this happened) and I'm beginning to feel the effects of the observation equivalent of tunnel vision. Close concentration on a small range of activities is making me feel like a rabbit before a stoat, not exactly transfixed by his stare because he's busy ignoring me, but slightly discomfited. This does occur again from time to time and I learn a trick of deliberately widening my field of vision for short periods. This results in my spending three days in a state of intimacy with another subject before making the shattering discovery that he is left handed! I had been too busy waiting for him to stop writing so that I could start recording to notice which hand was holding the biro.

John has moved into his characteristic pre-departure routine which comes to be my home-time signal. He compiles a set of papers on an imminent meeting for overnight reading, confirming the impression that he prepares for meetings more carefully than most social services staff. We exchange friendly goodbyes and he heads for home. I return to the hotel with a mass of data and some relief that all has gone smoothly; I'm looking forward to the next day of observation. Whether John will be looking forward to his next day after he phones the second councillor tonight and discovers that the counter-report has been widely distributed, only he can say. I forgot to ask.

2. What's going on here anyway?

This account of my first day as a professional observer was written soon after the event. Now, 13 years later, I am still being asked the same basic questions about doing observation. How much can you learn from watching people at work (or at play)? How much can you actually see and what conclusions can you draw from it all? Do people behave normally when they are being watched and do they react against it? And, more generally, what part can observation play in investigating library and information work?

To start with a fairly sweeping response to the last question, observation is important because there isn't anything else. All methods of investigation ultimately depend upon observation, whether this is in the form of direct measurement, asking people to reflect on their own experience and respond, or watching and recording other people. However, observation alone is not enough. The results have to be recorded in some way and organized for communication (usually in writing). One way of doing this is described below.

The observation session described in the opening paragraphs of this chapter was carried out as part of a major five-year study of information needs and information services in local authority social services departments, known as Project INISS. When we came together as a team of five researchers with different backgrounds (in 1975) we started from the more or less true assumption that we did not really know how or why social workers and their managers used information in their work, and this in a team which included a former social services administrator and another person who had undergone a social administration course with a strong social work element.

The obvious answer to this dilemma was to go and ask – but to ask what precisely? We were well aware that people find it difficult to discuss what information they want in a specific situation and what use they make of the information they have, even before we move on to the more abstruse area of 'information need'. Our work led us to reject the concept of 'information need' as unhelpful because it disguised the information and the process of communication which may or may not be helpful in responding to people's real affective (or emotional) and cognitive needs. If we were going to explore the 'information world' of social workers and their managers in any real depth it was clear that asking questions would be an important task, but asking questions that were likely to mean something to the people we were quizzing, ones that they would be able to answer and ones that would, in turn, have some meaning for us. In order to reach this level of understanding we felt the need to find out more about the world of the social worker by more direct means.

In an earlier attempt to describe the pros and cons of structured observation we presented two other reasons for building on our preparatory research reading with direct observation. From discussions prior to the research being funded it was evident that social services staff were unlikely to respond favourably if the initial approach used either interviews or self-completed questionnaires because they felt over-exposed to these research tools. It was felt desirable that the research team should establish credibility within a number of departments before attempting to use these methods; and it was evident that internal documents, research papers and other publications could not reveal all the nuances of organizational life and it was felt that a period of observation would reveal at least some of the unreported detail.[1]

This line of reasoning led us into a programme of direct observation of 22 individuals, ranging in status from director to basic grade social worker and administrative officer, in five social services departments, for periods of one week each. This work was followed by a phase of structured interviews in four departments and an 'action research' phase of the project in which various ideas for improving the utilization of information (mostly derived from the observation phase of the project) were field-tested in different departments.

We chose to adopt a method of 'structured observation' based on an approach used earlier by Henry Mintzberg[2] in his investigation of the managerial roles (including information roles) performed by chief executives in five North American organizations. The 'structure' in our case was imposed by the aims of the research in the same way the other research methods are fashioned to meet the needs of the researcher. Our approach entailed recording (on edge-notched 8" × 5" pre-printed cards) within various predetermined categories. These were:

- time (i.e., start and stop time of the discussion topic);
- source/receiver (i.e., people invoived in the discussion or activity);
- channel of communication (oral, telephone, writing, read-

ing, circulating information);
- medium of communication (e.g., one-to-one meeting; memo, letter, book);
- location of event (i.e., which office, etc.);
- content of message;
- response;
- remarks.

The last three categories were treated somewhat differently. In practice it was often difficult (and probably unimportant) to decide who had initiated a conversation and the 'response' tended to be subsumed within the detailed record of the discussion or item of information that constituted the 'content of message'. Most of the observation recording was concentrated on this category and subsequent analysis went well beyond the predetermined structure in assessing the activities engaged in while communicating and the purpose of the communication (as far as it could be surmised), including the most dominant work-role being performed. The remarks category was used to record any unusual features of the observation or other factors seen as relevant by the observer.

Using a ring-binder full of cards proved to be a fairly efficient means of recording except during hectic meetings or in difficult surroundings (such as a crowded pub). Under these circumstances the observer resorted to a notepad and transcribed the notes onto cards when time allowed.

Since a team of five observers was to be used, we decided at the outset that some observer training was necessary to ensure a level of consistency in recording activities. Two kinds of training were adopted. First, the use of a training film on communication as providing generalized and common ground for the observers. The film was shown to all five observers, the resulting records were compared and discussion took place on anomalies, missed 'events' and so on as a means of arriving at a common understanding of definitions. The film was then shown again to resolve any further issues. Secondly, all observers carried out trial observation periods of one or two days on members of staff in the university department where the project was based. Following the pilot field tests, further discussions were held to resolve problems and arrive at a common recording method.

Few real difficulties occurred once the observers moved into the field. This was partly because care had been taken to prepare the way by holding preliminary meetings with our subjects before each of the five observation weeks. Subjects were questioned about their education, experience, working habits and views on information, and operational arrangements for the observation week were made. Subjects were asked to obtain prior clearance for their observers to attend scheduled meetings and to alert their colleagues to our presence so that we would not be mistaken for visiting clients. Once observation had started there were very occasional problems in keeping up with a discussion, in understanding what was going on, or in catching part of the communication (for example, if someone forgot to relay the gist of the other end of their telephone conversation) but a brief question to the subject was usually enough to put this right. End of day review sessions were held with the other observers and provided the chance to ensure that records were complete.

At the end of each observation week a short de-briefing session was held to find out the subject's view of the week and reactions to being observed. Over the next month or so a narrative account of the week was prepared by the observer and sent to the subject. This formed the basis of the final interview in which subjects were asked whether the narrative account accurately reflected the events of the week; whether the generalizations drawn about their information behaviour were accurate; and whether the week described was fairly typical of their normal working week at that time. Any matters requiring clarification were raised and progress reports were obtained on any unresolved major issues of the week. Respondents were again asked about their experience of being observed.

Reports were then prepared for each department and the narrative accounts formed the basis of a published 'Week in the life of a social services department'[3] as well as providing the core statistics for further analysis. The feedback from the observation subjects was vital in clarifying issues and in supporting a range of emerging ideas about the information-related behaviour of social services staff, which were then tested in interviews before forming the basis of a set of published recommendations about improving social services communication.[4]

3. Answering some questions
Reverting to the earlier set of basic questions, how much can be learned from watching people at work (or in performing other roles)? This gives rise to another basic question: What is observation? In a useful little guide to the subject, Christine Mullings (one of the Project INISS team) offered a definition:

Observation is a way of collecting data in a purposeful and systematic manner about the behaviour of an individual or a group of people at a specific time and place. The purpose is to discover meaningful relationships and actions, either to support hypotheses or with a completely open mind. Observation usually takes place in a person's natural surroundings – at work, at school, using a library, etc. – and is carried out by watching and listening to the 'subject' of one's interest and recording what is happening .... Observation studies events as they actually occur and also what people do rather than what they say they do .... Observation can be used to study both users and usage.[5]

Leaving aside the debating point about what constitutes an open mind, it is clear that this definition takes us beyond the world of the researcher-observer and properly offers the technique to all those who would like to find out more about how people use information and information services. To give only a few recent examples, observation has been used by students and practising librarians or information officers to learn about the use of library catalogues, to plan the layout of library buildings, to locate an information service physically within an organization and to study the interaction between users and staff at reference enquiry points. Only the last of these investigations was carried out by a 'proper' researcher, a postgraduate student.[6]

How much can be learned by using this method? The Project INISS team concluded that structured observation is a highly appropriate method of moving beyond what people think you want to know and gathering basic information about how, when and why information is used in organizations. This is especially true in organizations which feature considerable face-to-face or telephone communication and heavy fragmentation of work. It was interesting to find that nearly all the ideas for improving social services communication developed by Project INISS originated in observation rather than in the later phases of the project.

Viewed from the perspective of library and information service practitioners, systematic observation offers possibilities for learning more about the information-related behaviour of potential users, which should in turn lead to the design of more effective services. An example of the practical application of this notion was the development of the Education Management Information Exchange (EMIE) service for local authority education officers and advisers. Observation of a small number of education officers at work led eventually to the formation of a service based on their three characteristic responses when faced with the necessity to obtain information about what was going on outside their department (see below). This observation work revealed a number of key elements of the behaviour of education officers which were later confirmed through discussion with many more of their colleagues. Since a similar approach was adopted to the one used by Project INISS it was also possible to compare the ways of working of social services managers and staff with those of the education officers.

Although the three education officers observed were doing different jobs and were at various levels of seniority, they (and their colleagues with whom they were in contact during observation) shared a number of characteristics of interest for the design of EMIE information services:

1.   Their work was fragmented with frequent interruptions, changes of topic and different participants in their communications.

2.   They disposed of most documents and publications received in a very short time, particularly when their contact with this written material only involved reading (as opposed, for example, to referring to a document in a discussion or writing a report based on documents).

3.   Most of the information events were conducted through oral (face-to-face or telephone) channels.

4.   They all spent substantial amounts of time in previously scheduled meetings.

5.   They showed no tendency to engage in systematic and protracted searching for information on matters of current concern.

6.   They evinced interest in the approaches other LEAs had taken to their own current problems.

7.   They tended to seek information or advice by contacting colleagues in their own or other departments, usually through oral channels.

8.   They showed readiness in responding to requests for information or advice in this way.

9.   They made little use of formal information stores apart from department files.

In all these characteristics the education officers were similar in their behaviour to the social services department managers observed by Project INISS. Some differences were, however, detected. The work of the education officers was even more fragmented than the average for social services staff (74% of information events were over in three minutes or less, compared with 62% for social services staff) and the average time spent by the education officers in reading documents and publications (84% took one minute or less) was shorter than for the social services managers (72%). Two more differences were noted:

10. The span of responsibility held by the LEA staff tended to be narrower than that of corresponding levels of staff in social services departments, reflecting the larger size and greater complexity of education department work.

11. The process of directly 'feeding into the policy-making pool' appeared to involve a larger proportion of LEA staff, at least intermittently.[7]

All these characteristics were taken into account in building up the EMIE service. In particular, great emphasis was placed upon identifying and using people (especially other education officers) as contacts for enquirers as well as rapidly providing a careful selection of key documentation (again largely derived from LEAs) and a summary of the 'state of play' in relation to the topic being explored. This special emphasis was adopted because education officers were seen to rely heavily on the contact network and on any documentation that met the immediate purpose when seeking information from outside their department. They also relied upon the regional and national activities of their professional association, the Society of Education Officers, to build up and maintain their contact network and to keep them in touch with significant changes in the education world. This led EMIE to seek a very close working relationship with the SEO.

Space does not allow further elaboration here about how the EMIE service was built up from the foundation of observation, but all concerned are convinced that the structured observation phase was a vital first step both in generating ideas and in establishing credibility with the clients.

Structured observation is only one variation on the observation technique, but one which seems highly appropriate to the library and information work field. At its simplest, systematic observation can begin with anyone watching other people. Even a limited amount of time spent in watching clients using a service, for example, may prove illuminating, especially if this approach is backed up by other methods of information gathering (such as interviews or statistical analysis of service use).

It is still relatively uncommon for observation to form a major part of library and information research, partly no doubt because it is a time-intensive and expensive process. However, observation has been used to great effect by social scientists concerned with other issues and in doing so this approach has sometimes shown information use to be a key factor in the topic studied. A good example of this approach is provided by John Johnson, a leading American sociologist, who went as a participant observer to a child welfare service office. The resulting study of 'The social construction of official information' [8] is likely to be of interest to anyone seriously concerned with how service organizations operate and how the workers use information in the political climate engendered in such organizations. Johnson also wrote one of the best books on the realities of doing participant observation. [9]

Incidentally, much space has been expended in the research literature on distinguishing between various forms of participant and non-participant observation. In practice, most library and information research-related observation is likely to be structured and non-participant in character, if only because the researcher will be concerned to capture information on who is talking to whom about what in a systematic manner and to record what information is being communicated. This won't leave much time for participation!

4. What do you see?

How much can you see in observation and what conclusions can you draw about it? The amount that can be observed will obviously depend upon the physical circumstances but, with the collaboration of an observation 'subject' it is possible to view most of what is going on in the person's office, at a meeting, etc. The extent to which the activity observed is comprehensible will depend upon the amount of preparation undertaken as well as the observer's general understanding of the organization or setting. As noted earlier, it is even possible to follow most telephone conversations by listening to one end of the conversation (although the subject's help in relaying the gist of the other part is usually sought). There are dangers, however, in assuming that your interpretation of events is accurate and reliable, as Tom Stoppard showed in his hilarious play *After Magritte*, where the progression from simple observation to the bizarre was performed effortlessly and with bewildering variations.

These dangers are likely to be compounded when the observer moves from recording events to describing them and drawing conclusions about, for example, their significance in designing information services. Fortunately, there is usually no need to rely on the unsupported testimony of the observer, and sensible research design will ensure that, whenever possible, the observation subjects and other people in the same general category have a chance to comment on the observer's views. Two obvious approaches are to check out the account and any conclusions with the person observed and to use observation as a basis for designing questionnaires or interviews to test the emerging ideas more systematically.

The likelihood that an observer will be excluded from seeing particular meetings or documents will vary enormously according to the setting, but experience has shown that trusted outsiders may be admitted to a surprising range of events and activities.

5. The watchers and the watched

Does observation interfere with the work being watched? Again, the answer will depend on the setting but some types of work are also more suitable for observation than others. To summarize a number of points made in an earlier account,[1] the method is probably *inappropriate*:

(a) if staff are largely desk-bound and have little supervisory responsibility involving informal oral contact;

(b) if staff spend lengthy periods engaged in one activity, such as report writing;

(c) if the status of the observers imposes a threat to the subjects, either because there is some implicit judgement of their performance involved or if they are seen as 'insiders' who are likely to profit from the information obtained, to the disadvantage of the subjects;

(d) and possibly, if staff are unused to being watched at work, although this is an untested assertion.

Individual responses to being observed will, of course, vary. One of the education officers observed for the EMIE project found the presence of the observer distracting but one of the others found the process enjoyable because it enabled her to reflect on what she was doing, even if she didn't feel the need to explain a particular point to the observer.

Most of the Project INISS 'victims' reported feeling an initial period of awareness of being observed, lasting between a few minutes and the whole of the first morning of observation, but they all became accustomed to the experience and in many cases appeared to become largely oblivious to the fact that they were being watched. The ideal preparation activity for the observation week seemed to be one or more meetings during the opening morning, because subjects who were engaged in early meetings appeared to relax more quickly under observation (presumably because their attention was focused on the other participants). After the opening day of observation only one subject, a research officer, appeared to be uncomfortable under observation, when he spent periods of up to four hours in assimilating documents and preparing reports. When not engaged in this sort of activity he appeared to behave in a 'normal' manner.

Observation subjects were encouraged to comment about the experience of being observed both at the end of the week and in subsequent interviews. Typical comments included:

'I enjoyed the attention . . .' (several other subjects claimed that they enjoyed the experience).

'It wasn't so bad as anticipated. I came back off leave and certainly didn't feel that I wanted anything else round my neck. I was pleasantly surprised.' When interviewed later this respondent added, 'It was much as I said to you. It was not as bad as I thought, it was surprisingly easy to be natural, surprisingly uninhibiting.'

'I got used to being observed as time went on.'

There was no discernible evidence (apart from one overdue meeting suddenly scheduled) to suggest that observer presence significantly altered people's behaviour. Indeed, the daily work pressure, the high degree of fragmentation in the work of all individuals observed and the frequent interaction with other people would have made any attempt to maintain a false pattern of behaviour extremely difficult.

To summarize the whole observation process from the Project INISS staff perspective, all the observers felt that the experience provided real insights into the way in which the work was done and the contribution which information made to that work. The activity was valuable as a learning experience for the observers and, in particular, proved stimulating in terms of generating ideas about communication in these organizations.

6. OK, now what?

Apart from taking its place as a phase in a major research project, observation can be used to effect in at least two other ways. Assuming that the general intention in engaging in systematic observation is to learn enough to be able to affect the situation being studied, it is clear that observation can usefully form part of an action research strategy.

Action research is a term applied to a fairly wide range of

different forms of intervention or interference in organizations. Here, I have assumed that the action research model is designed to improve performance or contribute to group understanding of an organizational problem. In this approach, the area of difficulty is defined by the researchers and practitioners together, before this problem is examined using appropriate methods which may well include observation. The results are then fed back to the participants who may choose to modify their practice in the light of what is presented to them. This cycle, including appropriate observation focused on the more specific area of concern identified in discussion, may be repeated several times until a satisfactory state has been reached or the participants have lost interest or otherwise been diverted into other areas. A variation on this approach is to involve the participants as observers in their own activity. One thriving area in which this way of working is habitually adopted is in classroom research, where groups of teachers meet regularly, investigate classroom issues of concern to them and act on the results.[10]

Another general approach seeks to capitalize on the fragmented nature of the manager's working week (not a feature peculiar to social services staff or education officers, according to the management literature). Such a working lifestyle allows little or no time for systematic reflection on what the managers are doing, including how they are managing information in their work. Indeed, the constant interruptions, changes of pace and theme that fragment the work of many managers make it very hard to see any job as a whole and to draw out appropriate lessons.

One way of overcoming this difficulty is to provide short (day or half-day) training opportunities on broad themes, with the emphasis on taking time out to reflect and to compare experiences with colleagues rather than on learning a particular skill. One such general theme may well be information management or 'improving communication in your organization', or whatever else has arisen from observation of information-related behaviour likely to be of interest to the manager. A similar sort of approach may also work with other groups, such as academic staff or headteachers.

The experience of the Project INISS and EMIE project work in this area has been described elsewhere.[11] Courses for managers have been successfully offered through the National Institute for Social Work and the Society of Education Officers. They have proved valuable in:

(a) providing a forum for the consideration of observation findings by practitioners;
(b) obtaining confirmation, amplification and clarification of some of the generalizations presented;
(c) giving the participants sufficient impetus to enable them to further examine their own information-related behaviour;
(d) allowing the airing of problems in obtaining, storing and exploiting information;
(e) facilitating group problem-solving around these issues;
(f) giving an appropriate way in to consideration of inform-ation technology as an information management tool rather than as an end in itself; and
(g) providing the researchers/organizers with a rich vein of further research-related information.

At its most effective, this sort of partnership approach to training, based on: 'This is what we saw; help us to explain it' not on: 'This is how you should do it', can lead to a substantial pooling of ideas, insight and knowledge. One example was the publication produced at the end of such a cycle of courses starting with 'communication problems' and ending with 'IT management'.[12]

Whatever the approach taken to the dissemination of observation findings it is clear that systematic observation is an important tool for the reflective and self-reflective manager or information worker.

References

1 Wilson, T. D., and Streatfield, D. R., 'Structured observation in the investigation of information needs', *Social science information studies*, 1, 1981, 173–84.

2 Mintzberg, H., *The nature of managerial work*, New York, Harper and Row, 1973 (2nd edition 1981).

3 Wilson, T. D., and Streatfield, D. R., *You can observe a lot ... a study of information use in local authority social services departments*, University of Sheffield, 1980 (See chapter two).

4 Streatfield, D. R., and Wilson, T. D., *The vital link: information in social services departments*, London, Community Care and the Joint Unit for Social Services Research, 1980.

5 Mullings, C., *CRUS Guide: 7. Observation*, University of Sheffield, Centre for Research on User Studies, 1984.

6 Barnes, M., *The relationship between public library staff and users: implications for service effectiveness, in-service training and public relations*, PhD Thesis No. 4888 University of Sheffield, Postgraduate School of Librarianship and Information Science, 1981.
   For another example of systematic observation by a researcher see: Fearn, M., *Promotional activities and materials for children in an urban*

branch library, Loughborough, Centre for Library and Information Management, 1982.

7 Streatfield, D. R., 'Moving towards the information user: some research and its implications', *Social science information studies*, **3**, 1983, 223–40.

8 Johnson, J. M., *The social construction of official information*, Ann Arbor, University Microfilms, 1974.

9 Johnson, J. M., *Doing field research*, New York, Free Press, 1975.

10 Sanger, J. (ed.), *Teaching, handling information and learning*, LIR Report 67, London, British Library Research and Development Department, 1989.

11 Streatfield, D. R., 'Consulting with the information user: a problem-based training approach', *in* Harris, C., and Taylor, P. (eds.), *Prospects for information service: essays in honour of Daphne Clark*, London, Aslib, 1985.

12 Streatfield, D. R., and Foreman, D., *Making IT work: managing computer-aided administration in LEAs*, Slough, NFER, 1987.

Acknowledgement

Most of the ideas presented in this chapter were developed in collaboration with Prof. Tom Wilson and other Project INISS colleagues. Their help is gratefully acknowledged.

10 Communicating the findings and publicizing the research

Jane Steele and Sue Ells

1. Introduction: The importance of effective communication in research

Good communication is essential to good research. From the outset, the research project depends heavily on a high standard of communication, right through to the final presentation of the findings and recommendations.

While many people realize the importance of a good final report, too few realize that the skills needed for that report need to be applied from the word go.

There are two aspects of good communication in research. One surrounds the area of publicity for the project; its aims and objectives etc. The other lies within the actual methodology – the quality of communication in questionnaires and reports etc.

In this chapter we will be looking at both of these, including why research needs good communication, how that can be achieved, and at which points in the process it should be happening. We will also be looking at how the ingredients for a well communicated project will vary, according to the type of project and the audience at which the findings are directed. In addition we will be looking at how effective project management can make the process of communication easier for the researcher.

In summary, this is the format in which we will be dealing with communication in research in this chapter:

- Why should communication in research be good?
- At which points in the project should communication be happening and with whom?
- What are the ingredients for good communication in a research project?
- How do we get the message across?
- Who are we talking to?
- Collecting the information for communication: how can good project management facilitate clear communication?

2. Why should communication in research be good?

Research is generally a means to an end. Research is the tool that is used to examine a situation and to supply findings for analysis so that recommendations for change can be made if and when necessary.

The success of this process relies greatly on the ability of the researcher to establish a good communication network for the project. In most research projects, researchers are dependent on people in the project environment providing them with accurate information. To facilitate this process, researchers need to make it clear: (a) what they are asking and also (b) what they are offering in return. The quality of the information collected in a research project should be as high as possible. The more reliable the information going into a research project, the more reliable the recommendation coming out at the other end will be.

It is important for researchers to remember throughout the project that they owe something to the people who contribute to the information they collect as well as to those people who are waiting for the final report and recommendations. All too often researchers seem to focus on the body who commissions the research report and pays the bills rather than those people who actually contribute to the information on which the research is based. These are the people who spend time sharing experiences and thoughts with the researcher. There are many ways however in which we can thank them. For example, we could offer them a copy of any final report and recommend-ations (where this is possible, bearing in mind the interests of the commissioning body). We could also offer these people some kind of group feedback in return for their participation. Projects which have built into them a reward (financial or otherwise) for respondents are very rare. If researchers can offer such 'thank you's' for participation at the start of any project then they should be able to encourage participation and also make people feel they have a small obligation to offer the best information they can. What the researcher needs to avoid is making assumptions that people are there to be researched and should participate in a project because they've been asked. This is the case even if these suppliers of information are employees of an organization which has itself commissioned a piece of research.

While talking about the obligations of a researcher, we should also talk about the obligations in terms of sharing knowledge of their work right from the word go. If as researchers we want to approach people and ask them for information, we should make sure they know why we are asking them. For this reason, we should make the effort to ensure that everybody who contributes knows what the research project is about, who is commissioning it, and what its long-term aims are. In being open and honest from the start, as far as the project allows, we are fulfilling our obligations as researchers and encouraging those contributing to the project to be open and honest with us.

Surprisingly enough, good clear communication in these areas is not a dominant feature of every research project. It is amazing how many researchers get so caught up in the idea of collecting information that they completely forget to give any out themselves; only focusing on the report at the end of the day which goes to the commissioning body. Yet by the very nature of research, researchers are essentially shooting themselves in the foot if they fail to communicate effectively from the start, as they are not doing their best to encourage contributions to the project.

Clear communication with participants in a research project is just as important as clear communication with a commissioning body. It is essential that once a research project has been proposed, all interested parties know exactly what has been proposed. Similarly, keep people informed about what is happening during the course of a research project, and make sure that everybody knows exactly what has happened at the end. Any recommendations for action need to be based clearly in findings. (The link between findings and recommendations should not have to be imagined by the interested parties!)

Given that research is generally a means to change, communication at the end of a project should be crystal clear. There are a variety of methods for presenting research findings. A written report is not necessarily the best way. Options in this area will be discussed later in the chapter.

To summarize, we have looked at the reasons why communication in research should be good. We have looked at our obligations to contributors, as well as to those commissioning a project. We have also looked at the need to convey exactly what has been found in a project clearly and the link to what is being recommended as a result of a project. A useful model to bear in mind when thinking about how clear communication around research projects should be is that of a recipe. As far as possible, all through a project from the beginning to the end, a researcher should be able to explain exactly what is going on so that anybody could replicate their project. The details should be similar to a recipe or a blueprint. Very few research projects fall apart because the researcher communicated too well or too much. Far too many research projects crumble because important information is not passed on to those that need to know.

Suspicion is another problem that the researcher frequently has to face. Researchers are often seen as a strange and rare breed. Few people are sure what they actually do. In the absence of clear communication about what they are doing at any particular instance, people are inclined to let their imagination run riot. This can be particularly harmful in some environments and organizations, and where a researcher is dependent on contributions.

3. At which points in the project should communication be happening and with whom?

Good communication is important *around* the research tools themselves, as well as being important *within* the research tools. Most researchers put in considerable time and effort to the construction of research tools like questionnaires and interview schedules, knowing that clear communication here is very important. Bear in mind, however, that the communication *around* these tools (such as explaining to people what you are going to be doing in the course of your research) is equally vital.

Already, as we have just seen, clear communication is essential throughout the research project. There are however distinct identifiable points at which most projects should be emitting information.

The first of these is obviously at the proposal stage. Once an idea for a project has been put together, it needs to be put down explicitly on paper so that it can be communicated to other people for comments. Proposals for research projects rarely become operational in their first draft state. Based on the comments of potential participants, a commissioning body, or experts in the field for example, most proposals go through several drafts. To enable this to happen, an initial draft needs to be produced and comments on it need to be actively sought.

The next major piece of information people need to know is when the project is actually happening. A provisional timescale for the project would be useful, not just for those commissioning the research but also for those participating. If you can tell people when you think you are going to be asking for information this will help them to make time available to you. This is better than knocking on someone's door unannounced and expecting them to have time for you there and then.

Communicating findings need not necessarily happen at the

end of a project. Action research for example is based on the principle of feeding back into a project findings as they are collected. This means that change can happen *within* the project, and need not have to wait until the end. In this kind of project, communication needs to be a continuous process between the researcher and the contributors to the project. Even in non-action research, people are more likely to continue to give you information if you are able to feed back your findings to date. This will give them the confidence that you are using what has been given so far. It will also encourage them to make points they feel are important, if it seems you haven't yet collected their particular views. When the researcher has collected all the information that is apparently necessary for the project and then disappears to do analysis and draw conclusions, things shouldn't go quiet. Contributors to the project should realize this is what is happening. They should also know when to expect further communications.

Finally there is the concluding report. This is an obvious place for clear communication. Contributors as well as commissioners will need to know outcomes and recommendations at this point. They will also need to know if further research appears to be necessary and the form that it might take.

So what we have done in this section is basically to conclude that clear communication should take place throughout the research project. However, we have identified the usual points at which a researcher would be communicating to participants and to commissioners. In the next section, we will be looking at the factors that make for good communication in research.

4. What are the ingredients for good communication in a research project?

The four main ingredients for good communication are:

- information
- language
- timing
- distribution networks.

The most obvious ingredient is information. Researchers should be clear about the information they are trying to convey, bearing in mind intended audiences. This particular point is important because not everyone involved in a research project will need or want the same information. Information should be relevant to the person receiving it. If it is not, the researcher runs the risk of the audience switching off before the project has even begun. Think about what people need to know. You should be giving enough information to clarify the situation for the recipient, yet not so much that he or she has to wade through it and decide what is relevant. By making it easier for recipients through pre-selection, it will be easier to ensure that the message is received.

Another important ingredient for good communication is appropriate language. In the same way that not all information is relevant to all participants in the project, not all sorts of language are appropriate for all sorts of participants. By language we don't just mean whether they speak Punjabi or Gujerati for example, we are also talking about levels of language. In some research projects, the people the researcher deals with will be used to, and indeed expect, communication to be in a language which is at quite a 'high' level and possibly contains a certain amount of jargon (for example the legal profession). On the other hand, the researcher may well find that participants need to be communicated with very differently, for example primary school children.

So, having decided upon the importance of communication and then on the information that you want to communicate, careful thought should be given to the language of that communication.

The timing of any communication is also important. It will help people to help you if they know what is happening when in a project. We mentioned earlier about the importance of preparing people to give information – warning them that you will be asking them for some time to help you with your investigations. If you can warn people that a research project will involve certain sorts of communications at certain times, as far as you can estimate, you will be helping them to assist you. Imagine, for example, that you are evaluating a new computer system over three months. You tell participants in the study that you will be contacting them during the last week of each month to see how they are getting on. It is likely that they will note any comments and thoughts they have and will be prepared in advance to discuss them with you on the arranged time. In this way they will have the chance to prepare their information for you.

Another important aspect of communication is the establishment of a clear communication network. Participants in a research project should know how to contact you if necessary, just as you should be able to contact them.

In many cases, if you can standardize this network so much the better. For example, you might establish a standard way of feeding back information over a period of time to participants through a newsletter. (It would be worth standardizing the timing of this communication too!)

It might also help if you can facilitate communication between participants. This will depend on the nature of the research project (in some cases you might actively wish to prevent this).

To summarize, the distribution network, timing and language of information to be communicated should all be given careful consideration.

5. How do we get the message across? – Tools to use

Nearly all research projects need to use a number of different tools of communication. The choice of tools to use depends on the following:

- length and size of the project
- nature of the research
- audience for the communication
- stage reached in the research.

Communications can be written or spoken. This part of the chapter is intended to help the researcher choose from a list of both types of tools by explaining for each:

- when it is appropriate
- how to use it.

5.1 *Written communications*

5.1.1 *Project brief*

A project brief is an essential tool for almost all research projects. It outlines very briefly, usually on one side of A4, the aims and objectives of the research, the reasons for the research, the methodology, the timescale and the names, addresses and telephone numbers of the researchers. This piece of paper can then be used to inform a wide range of people about the project – to inform people whom the researchers want to know about the project and to send out in response to any enquiries. For example, it can be sent out with letters requesting people to contribute to the research. Once the project gets underway the production of the project brief should be one of the earliest tasks to be done.

A project brief serves a second useful purpose. The process of drawing up the project brief is an excellent method of ensuring that everyone involved in doing, funding or managing the research has a shared understanding of its aims and methods. This process makes everyone concerned focus on the purpose and nature of the project and can help to clear up any misunderstandings at an early stage. Once the project brief is produced it becomes a very useful document to refer to later in the project, when it is quite usual for the researcher to feel bogged down and to lose sight of the original objectives.

5.1.2 *Posters*
The project brief is one way of letting people know that the research is happening. In some cases it may also be appropriate to inform people through posters. If the researcher needs to communicate with a large number of people who pass through a limited number of locations, especially if these are people who cannot be contacted through the post, then posters can be very useful. For example, a research project that needs to involve the users of a library or information centre can inform the public that the research is happening by means of a poster or posters in a prominent place. Then, when individuals are approached to provide information for the research, they are to some extent prepared and may be more willing to participate. It can also be a useful public relations move to let people know that the organization is doing research to improve its services. Posters should be well designed, eye-catching and contain very brief information about the research – the reasons and the implications for the people reading it. The researcher should also think about the best methods for communicating with the particular audience. Would it be more appropriate to use languages other than English? Would graphic images or photographs be more effective than text?

5.1.3 *Newsletters*
Lengthy projects that need to keep people interested throughout their duration can benefit from production of newsletters for distribution to all the research participants and other interested parties. A newsletter can be used to inform participants of preliminary findings and thus help to maintain their interest and encourage them to continue their involvement. The newsletter can be brief, perhaps one side of A4, but if it is well presented and its content is directly relevant to the circumstances of the readers it can be invaluable in, for example, boosting the response rate to second and subsequent questionnaires in a project.

5.1.4 *Press releases*
In some instances the researchers will want to publicize their

work to a wider audience, either public or professional. This may happen at the beginning of the project, to announce that it is happening, and at the end, to publicize the results. Usually this happens with larger projects whose findings will be relevant to many different organizations. Such publicity can also be useful in making other organizations aware of the existence of the research team and its work.

The press release should be short, no more than one side of A4. It should begin with an eye-catching sentence to capture the interest of the editors reading it. It is much more likely to be used if it can easily be cut by an editor without losing any essential information. So make sure that the first paragraph encapsulates the total message of the press release. A name, telephone number and address for further information should always be included. When the press release is announcing the findings of a research project, details of the title, price and how to obtain the report should also be included.

The press release can be sent to specialist and popular journals. Where a researcher is likely to issue several press releases over a period of time it might be worth maintaining a press mailing list on a computer so that information can be updated and address labels produced with minimum effort. Also, it is worth checking whether other organizations or professional bodies in the field have mailing lists that can be bought or borrowed.

5.1.5 *Journal articles*
Many research projects produce results which can be used to generate research articles, but for reasons of ethics, confidentiality or politics it is not always appropriate to publish the work, even if the results would be of great interest to other people. However, for publishable work that is not solely concerned with an organization's internal affairs, the sharing of information about the results makes the research worth while, and journal articles are a very useful way of doing this. Journal articles reach a large audience, create a fairly permanent record of the work and are covered by indexing and abstracting services, which helps the information to be located by a greater number of people.

The researcher should think carefully about the target audience for the article and select the journals that are most likely to be read by that group of people. There may be several appropriate journals, in which case it is sensible to concentrate on two or three with different styles – there is no point in producing two very similar articles for similar journals which are likely to have the same readership. Having selected the journals, it is worth contacting the editors to find out whether they would be interested in an article and checking their rules about length, house-style etc.

5.1.6 *Reports*

Many books have been written on the topic of report-writing, some of which are listed at the end of this chapter. It is indeed a topic worthy of a whole book to itself and this section gives only brief guidance on when to produce the different sorts of report. Almost all research projects produce a final report but the format this takes and how it is distributed will vary from project to project. In addition there is often a need for interim and summary reports for different audiences.

Any project requiring more than a few months' work should build in the production of interim reports at, say, six-monthly intervals. The researchers may often feel that they do not have the time to set aside from the real business of doing the research to write such a report, but it can be a very useful exercise indeed. The writing of an interim report provides an opportunity to reflect on the work so far, and provides a basis for making any necessary adjustments to the plan for the rest of the project. When the researcher reaches the usual stage of feeling over-whelmed or disenchanted with the project, it can provide a welcome source of energy, as it demonstrates how much work has already been done and suggests what steps should follow.

The interim report is a useful tool of communication as it informs everyone concerned with the project (researchers, project managers and funders) about progress and the continuing programme of work. It can also help to clarify any problems before they become too serious. It is not unknown for a project to change its direction quite radically when an interim report has made it evident that the project as originally planned was not going to be appropriate. The interim report should be quite short, outlining the work completed, any preliminary findings, any issues for discussion and the plan for the next stage of the project.

Almost all research projects will be required to produce a final report which contains a full record of the work – the back-ground, aims and objectives, methodology, discussion and appendices (questionnaires, interview schedules etc.) as well as the results and recommendations. This report will be needed by the organization commissioning the research and can also be used to disseminate the results to a wider audience. However, the researcher should also consider whether there is a need for a shorter version of the report which explains the research and its implications to the wider audience without going into detail on the background, methodology and so on. It is important to assess with some care the likely size of the market or audience for a short report, when deciding whether or not it is worth investing the time and money in producing and publicizing it. A journal article may serve the same purpose.

5.2 *Spoken communications*

5.2.1 *Personal presentations*
It is often worth the researcher taking the time and trouble to do a personal presentation on the work to those people directly affected by it, either during the project or at the end when the conclusions have been drawn. A presentation can provide the researcher with the opportunity to get valuable information and feedback from the group and to dispel any misunderstandings or suspicion, where the research is seen as a potential threat. The researcher should also work on the assumption that most people will not read any of the project reports in detail. A personal presentation can give them the gist of the contents and make sure they have got the message that the researcher wants to convey. This can be true even of a project steering committee or project funders, particularly where a report is long or raises some complex or unexpected issues.

5.2.2 *Workshops, conferences and seminars*
Meetings of various sorts which bring together in one place a number of people who are concerned with the field of the research are an excellent opportunity to communicate information about the project and its results. As with other forms of spoken communication, they can provide immediate feedback and response to the researcher. If the event is well organized, it will also encourage the participants to get involved in discussion, thus stimulating their interest and perhaps the likelihood of their taking action on what they have heard.

As with all forms of communication outside the immediate group of people who are commissioning or participating in the research, the researcher needs to consider whether it is appropriate to give it wider publicity and whether this publicity will be of interest to a larger audience. If so the researcher should look at the possibility of either organizing an event or contributing to one that is being organized by someone else.

Organizing an event is a time-consuming business, but worth it if there is likely to be sufficient interest and the subject is sufficiently large or important to justify it. It can also be expensive, depending on whether or not the organizers think they can cover their costs by charging people to attend. The alternative is to look out for conferences on appropriate subjects which are likely to attract interested participants and to approach the conference organizers with a request to present a paper or hold a workshop.

5.2.3 *Radio, television, video*

A small proportion of research projects are likely to be of such wide public interest that they may be suitable for coverage on radio or television, in which case the researcher will need to be able to present the most important points about the research in just a few sentences.

Some research projects, notably those concerned with providing guidance on practical tasks to a group of people, may find video a useful way of communicating the results. Videos can then be used by trainers, for example, to inform staff about the research and its findings.

6. Who are we talking to?

As we have already touched on in previous sections, a great deal of thought should go into the audience of your communication. The researcher needs to think carefully about 'the nature of the need to know'. By this we are referring to the differing information needs of management, participants, consumers, funders/ providers and practitioners.

Different people will need to know different things from a research project. That applies to how the project is structured and run, as well as to what is found and recommended. This doesn't mean that certain groups should not receive information which is of primary use to other groups. It just means that the researcher should be aware of which aspects of information should be emphasized for which groups. For example, it is quite useful for consumers of a service to know how it is managed in general terms, though not in the kind of detail that interests the management themselves.

Having established the nature of the need to know, we need to consider level, content, language and amount.

You will need to decide on the level of information for members of your audience. These considerations will include whether it should be sophisticated and detailed or perhaps brief and chatty, for example.

The appropriate content of your information should also be influenced by your audience. Some might consider factual information to be of primary importance, while others may consider philosophical issues to be more relevant. This will be influenced by the nature of the project.

Once again we revert to the subject of language. You may find that your information has to be presented in more than one language as well as at different levels within those languages. The researcher should also be alert to the use of jargon and certain terminologies amongst different groups. While it is not safe to make assumptions about understanding of jargon, many specialists would find it abnormal to receive communications which habitually used long-winded terms.

Deciding on the amount of information to communicate is also crucial. Different groups will expect different amounts of knowledge. Different groups will also be able to handle different amounts of knowledge. Don't bore your audience. Try to determine what is the right amount of information and provide it to the best of your ability.

7. Collecting the information for communication

Having the right information to communicate necessarily depends on the researcher being well organized. Good project management isn't just for the benefit of funders and commissioners. It is useful at this point to outline a skeleton filing system. Obviously every researcher will develop their own system, but it should contain these main elements.

First of all two card-index boxes are needed. One of these is for references and the other is for contacts. In the reference box, write up a card for each book or title in the standard format and file in alphabetical order. This should be done from the very start of the project. This system has two main benefits. Firstly, once you get into the habit of carrying a few blank cards around with you, there is no reason why at the end of the day you should have to search around for details of items you remember reading and have good notes on, but can't quite remember the full bibliographic identification. Secondly, this system has the advantage that when it comes to typing any written report, the authors' names are in alphabetical order and details can be typed straight from the cards. The other box should be maintained throughout the project in the same way. Names of contacts and their addresses and telephone numbers should be kept, again in alphabetical order. Notes relating to the nature of the contact can be kept on the back of each card. This will provide a quick reference list and is handy to keep by the phone, so that when you get calls you can quickly check (in case you have forgotten!) who is calling and what contact you have already had with them.

Another essential tool is a project diary. This should also be kept from the very start of a project. The diary should contain brief details of events and contacts with times and dates. This could include dates when presentations of the project plan were made and details of persons or groups to whom they were made. It should also contain details of dates that any questionnaires were sent out, how many were sent, as well as dates when forms were returned. This is particularly useful when making a written report. It can also prove useful in the event of any queries being raised about the progress or methodology of the project. It is not unknown for research projects to unearth information during their course which suggests that the original project plan is no longer appropriate. In such a case, the diary can help to support any request to a commissioning body to agree to a change in the project plan mid-course. In addition to the quick reference system of the two card boxes and the project diary, you should have a comprehensive filing system. The filing system can be divided up into four main slots. These are:

- project contract and plan
- communications
- finances
- background information and references.

The first slot should contain the detail of the agreed project proposal and any contract that might have been signed. It is quite important to have this available for reference throughout the project, as it is easy to lose sight of the original agreed aims and objectives once you get immersed in the information gathering process. In this slot the researchers should also have their project plan and projected timescales. Again this may need to be referred to several times and it is quite likely that during the project other people will want to see it.

In the second slot copies of all communications should be kept. This section may be sub-divided into communications between the commissioning body and the researcher and communications between the participants and the researcher. All letters should be kept in date order and preferably put in one file so it is easier to see how matters develop.

The third slot needs to contain the financial information relating to the project. This may include details of funding or grants. It should include details about expenditure (e.g., travelling, printing, overheads etc.). It is also a good idea to keep receipts where possible. These should be filed in this section. Again it is useful to keep things in date order.

The fourth slot should contain any accumulated background information and references. It might well be that the researcher collects photocopies of relevant articles. In such cases, these can be cross-referenced on the card index to indicate that copies are held on file. Sources for each of these should be noted on the document.

In a final slot the researcher should keep copies of all originals. These are master copies of any questionnaires, circulars, newsletters etc. that have been used in the project. This is very useful for compiling any final written report, as copies of each item should feature in the appendices. It is also useful to know where originals are and be able to access them easily in case extra copies are needed (many projects involve staggered starts).

The format and size of any of these elements as project management tools will obviously vary with the size and nature of the project in hand. However, the basic principles remain the same. Carefully made records from the outset of a project can save a researcher an awful lot of headaches and worry later on. It is well worth putting some time and effort in at the start to save time and effort at the end.

Further reading

Duffy, T. (ed.), *Designing usable texts*, London, Bingley, 1985.

Felker, D., *et al.*, *Guidelines for document designers*, Washington DC, American Institute for Research, 1981.

Hartley, J., *Designing instructional text*, 2nd edn, London, Kogan Page, 1985.

Maher, C., and Cutts, M., *Writing plain English*, Salford, Plain English Campaign, 1980.

Moore, N., and Hesp, M., *The basics of writing reports*, London, Bingley, 1985.

Index

action research 148–65, 170
aims definition, objectives
  1–7, 48–9, 63, 111–15, 129–33
attitude measurement, scaling
  65–70, 123–5
averages 84–7

bias 26–7, 69–70, 115–16, 153,
  157, 160–2, 166–8
boxplots 89–90, 101

chi-square 94–7
closed questions 52–7, 65–9,
  71–2, 109–10
cluster sampling 29–31
communication 8, 57–8, 75,
  117–19, 146–7, 155, 166–80
computer analysis 11–21, 81–3,
  87–105, 135
confidence interval 33
content analysis 122–5, 128–47
correlation coefficient 35
critical incident 73

data reduction/presentation
  47–9, 83–7
design factor/effect in sampling
  34–6
desk research 9–22, 46–9,
  78–94, 97–105, 122–3
dialogic investigation 115,
  117–18, 137
diaries 123

exploratory data analysis (EDA)
  87–97

filing system, project records
  management 6–7, 121, 145,
  178–80

group discussions 112–15, 122,
  139

interviewing, interviews
  54–6, 60–1, 112–19, 133–4,
  136–9

multivariate analysis 104

newsletters 173

observation 50–2, 118–21,
  136–8, 148–65
online use survey 11–14
open questions 64, 73–4, 114,
  123–5, 128–47
oral presentations 8, 146–7,
  176–8

pilots 74–5, 155
plans, project briefs, proposals
  1–7, 169, 172–3, 179
posters 173
press releases 173–4
projective techniques 123–6
purposive, non-probability
  and qualitative sampling
  40–2, 110–11, 134

qualitative analysis 121–5,
  128–47
qualitative survey methods
  107–27, 129–31, 133–9, 148–65
quantitative analysis 44–9,
  77–105
quantitative survey methods
  9–21, 44–61, 63–73, 107–10
questionnaire design 52–6,
  62–76, 112, 114
questionnaire surveys 52–61
quota samples 41

random samples 27–8, 31–6,
    97–101
recruiting, response rates
    26–31, 41, 53–4, 56–61,
    62–3, 73, 110–11, 171
reporting results 8, 121–2,
    146–7, 174–7

sample size 28, 36–8, 110, 134
samples, sampling 23–43,
    97–101, 110, 134
sampling error 31–6
sampling frames 38–40
sampling theory 23–31
scatterplots 91
self-completed questionnaires
    53–60

significance testing 90–7, 101–4
softback sales 79–95, 98–104
stemplots, leaf and stemplots
    87–8
stratified samples 28–9
survey population 23

t-test 102–4
tape recorders 114, 135–9
target population 23
telephone interviews 39,
    116–18
time series data 92–4

variables 77–81